R.L. Stine

WHO
WROTE
THAT?

LOUISA MAY ALCOTT

JANE AUSTEN

AVI

JUDY BLUME

BETSY BYARS

BEVERLY CLEARY

ROBERT CORMIER

BRUCE COVILLE

ROALD DAHL

CHARLES DICKENS

THEODORE GEISEL (DR. SEUSS)

WILL HOBBS

C.S. LEWIS

L.M. MONTGOMERY

GARY PAULSEN

EDGAR ALLAN POE

BEATRIX POTTER

PHILIP PULLMAN

MYTHMAKER: The Story
    of J.K. Rowling

SHEL SILVERSTEIN

R.L. STINE

EDWARD STRATEMEYER:
    Creator of the Hardy Boys
    and Nancy Drew

E.B. WHITE

JANE YOLEN

WHO WROTE THAT?

R.L. Stine

Hal Marcovitz

Foreword by
Kyle Zimmer

CHELSEA HOUSE
PUBLISHERS
A Haights Cross Communications ✦ Company ®
Philadelphia

CHELSEA HOUSE PUBLISHERS

VP, NEW PRODUCT DEVELOPMENT   Sally Cheney
DIRECTOR OF PRODUCTION   Kim Shinners
CREATIVE MANAGER   Takeshi Takahashi
MANUFACTURING MANAGER   Diann Grasse

STAFF FOR R.L. STINE

EXECUTIVE EDITOR   Matt Uhler
EDITORIAL ASSISTANT   Sarah Sharpless
PRODUCTION EDITOR   Noelle Nardone
PHOTO EDITOR   Sarah Bloom
INTERIOR AND COVER DESIGNER   Keith Trego
LAYOUT   21st Century Publishing and Communications, Inc.

A Haights Cross Communications Company ®

First Printing

1 3 5 7 9 8 6 4 2

Library of Congress Cataloging-in-Publication Data applied for.

Marcovitz, Hal.
    R.L. Stine/Hal Marcovitz.
       p. cm.—(Who wrote that?)
    Includes bibliographical references and index.
    ISBN 0-7910-8659-3
1. Stine, R. L.—Juvenile literature. 2. Young adult fiction—Authorship—
Juvenile literature. 3. Authors, American—20th century—Biography—Juvenile
literature. 4. Horror tales—Authorship—Juvenile literature. I. Title. II. Series.
PS3569.T4837Z775 2005
813'.54—dc22
                                                              2005008186

All links and Web addresses were checked and verified to be correct at the time
of publication. Because of the dynamic nature of the Web, some addresses
and links may have changed since publication and may no longer be valid.

Table of Contents

FOREWORD BY
KYLE ZIMMER
PRESIDENT, FIRST BOOK   6

1   MONSTERS IN THE ATTIC   11

2   MAKING A DREAM COME TRUE   21

3   JOVIAL BOB STINE   37

4   FROM FEAR STREET TO GOOSEBUMPS   51

5   R.L. STINE AND THE CRAFT
OF WRITING HORROR   63

6   STINE HEARS FROM HIS CRITICS   75

7   CENSORING GOOSEBUMPS   87

8   THE NIGHTMARE ROOM . . . AND BEYOND!   97

NOTES   106

CHRONOLOGY   110

MOST POPULAR BOOKS   111

WORKS BY R.L. STINE   113

MOST WELL-KNOWN CHARACTERS   120

MAJOR AWARDS   122

BIBLIOGRAPHY   123

FURTHER READING   125

WEBSITES   126

INDEX   128

FOREWORD BY
KYLE ZIMMER
PRESIDENT, FIRST BOOK

HUMANITY IS POWERED by stories. From our earliest days as thinking beings, we employed every available tool to tell each other stories. We danced, drew pictures on the walls of our caves, spoke, and sang. All of this extraordinary effort was designed to entertain, recount the news of the day, explain natural occurrences—and then gradually to build religious and cultural traditions and establish the common bonds and continuity that eventually formed civilizations. Stories are the most powerful force in the universe; they are the primary element that has distinguished our evolutionary path.

Our love of the story has not diminished with time. Enormous segments of societies are devoted to the art of storytelling. Book sales in the United States alone topped $26 billion last year; movie studios spend fortunes to create and promote stories; and the news industry is more pervasive in its presence than ever before.

There is no mystery to our fascination. Great stories are magic. They can introduce us to new cultures, or remind us of the nobility and failures of our own, inspire us to greatness or scare us to death; but above all, stories provide human insight on a level that is unavailable through any other source. In fact, stories connect each of us to the rest of humanity not just in our own time, but also throughout history.

This special magic of books is the greatest treasure that we can hand down from generation to generation. In fact, that spark in a child that comes from books became the motivation for the creation of my organization, First Book, a national literacy program with a simple mission: to provide new books to the most disadvantaged children. At present, First Book has been at work in hundreds of communities for over a decade. Every year children in need receive millions of books through our organization and millions more are provided through dedicated literacy institutions across the United States and around the world. In addition, groups of people dedicate themselves tirelessly to working with children to share reading and stories in every imaginable setting from schools to the streets. Of course, this Herculean effort serves many important goals. Literacy translates to productivity and employability in life and many other valid and even essential elements. But at the heart of this movement are people who love stories, love to read, and want desperately to ensure that no one misses the wonderful possibilities that reading provides.

When thinking about the importance of books, there is an overwhelming urge to cite the literary devotion of great minds. Some have written of the magnitude of the importance of literature. Amy Lowell, an American poet, captured the concept when she said, "Books are more than books. They are the life, the very heart and core of ages past, the reason why men lived and worked and died, the essence and quintessence of their lives." Others have spoken of their personal obsession with books, as in Thomas Jefferson's simple statement, "I live for books." But more compelling, perhaps, is the almost instinctive excitement in children for books and stories.

Throughout my years at First Book, I have heard truly extraordinary stories about the power of books in the lives of children. In one case, a homeless child, who had been bounced from one location to another, later resurfaced—and the only possession that he had fought to keep was the book he was given as part of a First Book distribution months earlier. More recently, I met a child who, upon receiving the book he wanted, flashed a big smile and said, "This is my big chance!" These snapshots reveal the true power of books and stories to give hope and change lives.

As these children grow up and continue to develop their love of reading, they will owe a profound debt to those volunteers who reached out to them—a debt that they may repay by reaching out to spark the next generation of readers. But there is a greater debt owed by all of us—a debt to the storytellers, the authors, who have bound us together, inspired our leaders, fueled our civilizations, and helped us put our children to sleep with their heads full of images and ideas.

WHO WROTE THAT? is a series of books dedicated to introducing us to a few of these incredible individuals. While we have almost always honored stories, we have not uniformly honored storytellers. In fact, some of the most important authors have toiled in complete obscurity throughout their lives or have been openly persecuted for the uncomfortable truths that they have laid before us. When confronted with the magnitude of their written work or perhaps the daily grind of our own, we can forget that writers are people. They struggle through the same daily indignities and dental appointments, and they experience the intense joy and bottomless despair that many of us do. Yet somehow they rise above it all to deliver a powerful thread that connects us all. It is a rare honor to have the opportunity that these books provide to share the lives of these extraordinary people. Enjoy.

An old typewriter that would-be author R.L. Stine found in the attic of his boyhood home in Ohio proved a hidden treasure. Using the old typewriter, 9-year-old Stine began writing material for short humor magazines and books.

1

Monsters in the Attic

BOB STINE STARTED making up scary stories when he was 7 years old and living in Bexley, Ohio, a suburb of Columbus. Stine shared a second-floor bedroom with his younger brother, Bill Stine, who is three years his junior. At night, the two brothers would lie in bed and stare at the ceiling, wondering what was in the attic above.

"What terrible thing is up there in the attic?" Stine would ask himself.[1] His never-ending curiosity stemmed from his mother's constant refusal to let him climb the stairs to explore the attic's musty contents. "It was strictly forbidden," Stine recalls. "Mom told us never to go up there. I asked her why. She only shook her head and said, 'Don't ask.'"[2]

And so, at night, after the two boys were sent up to bed Stine would let his mind wander. Since he wasn't allowed to explore the attic, Stine used his imagination to make up stories about what might be up there. He says:

> I pretended I could see through the plaster. Of course I couldn't see anything. Except plaster. But my imagination sure could. In my imagination, a coat rack stood at the top of the attic stairs. Next to it a three-legged table, several cardboard cartons, and an old windup record player. That dark shape in the corner was a mysterious, old trunk. Oh, and there was a dusty moose head. I could see this stuff as clear as day. But it was only furniture. It wasn't scary. The scary part was the monster in the attic. I made it up. And I made up stories about the monster with trunks and moose heads. These stories seem silly to me now, but at the time they were the best answer I could come up with to the question, *What's in the attic?*[3]

With Bill in the bed next to his, Stine couldn't resist the temptation to tell the stories he had made up about the attic. Stine's stories were full of ghosts, mummies, and werewolves—the type of mythical creatures he learned about when he tuned in his favorite shows on the radio. (This was in the early 1950s, when television sets were found in only a small number of American homes.) Stine loved shows that centered on crime and the supernatural. One such show was called *The Shadow*, which told stories about a sinister crime fighter who possessed the "power to cloud men's minds." He also enjoyed *The Whistler*, a crime show narrated by a mysterious character who called himself the Whistler. Each week, the creepy narrator would open the show by telling his audience, "I am the Whistler, and I know many things for I walk by night. I know many strange tales, many secrets hidden in the hearts of men and women who have stepped into the shadows. Yes, I know the nameless terrors of which they dare not speak." A third show Stine enjoyed was *Innersanctum*, which told eerie tales of ghosts and murderers. Each *Innersanctum* drama began with a spooky chord of organ music followed by the sound of a creaking door opening slowly. Stine says, "When I was a little kid I remember being real scared, lying in bed listening to these scary things on the radio. I loved that."[4]

Stine's all-time favorite program on the radio was the show *Suspense*. This was an enormously popular program; it remained on the air for 20 years. Indeed, *Suspense* had such a devoted audience that it was aired on the radio until 1962, well after television established itself as the primary source of home entertainment in America. Stine says, "In the beginning of the show, a long gong would chime. And then a very creepy announcer with a deep voice would say: 'And now . . . tales . . . calculated . . . to keep you in . . . SUSPENSE!' His voice was so terrifying, it gave me the chills."[5]

Stine was determined to prove that he could be just as scary as the Shadow, the Whistler, and the narrator who opened each of the *Suspense* programs. And so, just before the lights went off in the Stine brothers' bedroom, Stine would tell the creepiest stories he could imagine— determined to give his little brother a scare right before bedtime. Often the mysterious attic above the boys' bedroom would play an important role in the story. In many cases, Stine says, the story would open with an ugly green lizard-monster slithering out of the attic. According to Stine, a typical story would start like this:

The kid is in his room and he's terrified.

All he got was a glimpse of the thing. What is it? The boy doesn't know. It looked like a man, like a big, stooped man. But the head—it wasn't exactly a man's head. Men didn't have faces with fins and dripping lizard scales . . .

The kid can hear the footsteps. The thing is searching other bedrooms.

Where should the boy hide? He hasn't got much time.[6]

Did you know...

When R.L. Stine was a young boy his mother read him a story he found terrifying. Today, Stine claims that story is responsible for teaching him the meaning of true horror, whetting his interest for other frightening tales.

That story was *Adventures of Pinocchio*.

Most people are familiar with the story from the animated version produced by the Walt Disney Company. Pinocchio is a wooden puppet that is brought to life by a good fairy to provide companionship for the lonely woodcutter Gepetto. In the Disney movie version of the story there is plenty of singing and dancing, and in the end Pinocchio learns a moral lesson. He learns the importance of telling the truth, and it is this knowledge that earns him the right to become a real boy, no longer made of wood.

The original story, though, is much darker. In the original version, written in 1881 by Italian author

As then 4-year-old Bill listened to the story, eyes wide open, Stine would tell his brother about the lizard-monster chasing the hapless boy through the house. Finally, Stine told his brother, just as the boy thinks he has found a safe hiding place in the hall closet, he opens a door and:

> He is shocked by what he sees in the closet. Stunned! It's horrible. Gruesome. The kid starts to scream.[7]

Just at the point where Stine built the suspense up to the maximum, he would abruptly stop the story to tell his brother to turn out the light. Bill would protest loudly,

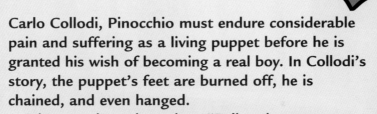

Carlo Collodi, Pinocchio must endure considerable pain and suffering as a living puppet before he is granted his wish of becoming a real boy. In Collodi's story, the puppet's feet are burned off, he is chained, and even hanged.

Stine says in an interview, "Believe it or not, my introduction to scary literature was *Pinocchio*. My mother read it to me every day before naptime when I was three or four. The original *Pinocchio* is terrifying. First he smashes Jiminy Cricket to death with a wooden mallet. Then he goes to sleep with his feet up on the stove and burns his feet off! I never forgot it!"*

* "An Interview With the World's Best-Selling Children's Author, R.L. Stine," R.L. Stine–HarperChildrens, *www.harperchildrens.com/catalog/author_interview_xml .asp?authorid=14471.*

As a boy growing up in Ohio, R.L. Stine was forbidden by his parents to go up in the attic of the family home. At night, he would make up scary stories to tell his younger brother about the monsters, ghosts, and other imaginary creatures that lived up there. Now, decades later, Stine is still making up stories about monsters in the attic.

crying that he wanted his older brother to finish, but even at the age of 7, Stine had discovered the value of a good cliffhanger. If Bill wanted to hear how the story ends, he would have to wait another night. "I would fall asleep with a cruel smile on my face, leaving my brother in total suspense," he says.[8]

Decades later, Stine is still making up stories about monsters in the attic. Only now, writing under the name R.L. Stine, his audience includes many more people than his little brother. In fact, millions of readers have helped make R.L. Stine the most successful author of young readers' fiction in history. His books in the Goosebumps, Fear Street, The Nightmare Room, Dangerous Girls, and Mostly Ghostly series have helped him sell more than 300 million books.

And even now, after authoring more than 400 books, Stine has never forgotten how truly creepy an attic can be. Indeed, it seems that whenever Stine needs a good place to start a scary story, he often finds himself relying on the attic. In *Piano Lessons Can Be Murder*, the thirteenth book in the Goosebumps series, the story opens on the day Jerry and his family move into a new house. As Jerry explores his new room, he opens what he believes is a door to a closet only to find that it leads to a "narrow, wooden stairway."[9] Of course, curiosity overwhelms Jerry and he scampers right up the attic stairs, ignoring all protests from his father. Disappointed, Jerry finds the attic to be all but empty—except for a large shape covered with a quilt. Jerry pulls the cover off to find an old piano. That night, while trying to fall asleep, Jerry hears piano music coming from the attic. He walks softly up the attic steps to investigate, but when he reaches the top he sees that there's nothing there.

Stine also visits the attic in the sixth Goosebumps book, titled *Let's Get Invisible*. This time, Max and his friends explore Max's family's attic in which they find a tall rectangular mirror. They soon find that anybody whose reflection is cast in the mirror turns invisible.

> Did I have a reflection?
>
> I turned and stared into the mirror. The light was pouring down from the top of the frame, casting a bright glare over the glass.
>
> Squinting into the glare, I saw . . . *nothing*.
>
> No me.
>
> No Lefty.
>
> Just a reflection of the wall behind us and the open door-way leading to the rest of the attic.[10]

Back at Stine's home in Bexley, he eventually worked up enough courage to explore his family's attic. One day, in defiance of his mother's orders, Stine opened the door to the attic and crept up the old, dusty stairs to finally see for himself whether it contained moose heads, trunks, and treasure chests. Much to his disappointment, he found little of interest—just some of his mother's out-of-style dresses and his father's old work clothes. Turning to leave the attic, though, Stine's eyes fell on an old black case sitting on the attic floor:

> "I walked over and picked up the case," he recalls. "It was coated with dust. The handle squeaked. I carried the case over to the stairs and sat down. There was a lock on the case. I snapped it open."[11]

Inside the case Stine found an old typewriter. He dragged the typewriter down from the attic. At the bottom of the stairs, Stine found his mother waiting for him, angry that he had defied her orders and explored the attic on his own. "I warned you about the attic," she told him. "The floors are rotting. It isn't safe."[12]

Stine was punished for disobeying his mother. But she did permit him to keep the typewriter. Soon, it would launch him on his career as a writer.

R.L. Stine grew up in Bexley, Ohio, a typical American small town located just outside the state capital of Columbus. Columbus is also the home of Ohio State University, which Stine would attend beginning in 1961.

2

Making a Dream Come True

ANYBODY SEARCHING FOR the typical American small town need only look as far as Bexley, Ohio. The community of Bexley is made up of some 13,000 residents and can be found four miles east of Columbus. The capital of Ohio, Columbus is home to 700,000 people as well as Ohio State University, one of the largest colleges in the United States. A visitor to Bexley won't find the hard urban streets or the exciting nightlife of a typical college town. Instead, Bexley is known for its farmer's market, which is open all summer, and its "Winter Market," an annual arts and crafts event held each

November that is designed to lure shoppers into Bexley's downtown areas.

Bexley is the town where Robert Lawrence Stine grew up. He was born on October 8, 1943, in Columbus, but moved to Bexley as a young boy. His father, Lewis Stine, worked as a shipping manager for a restaurant supply company. His mother, Anne Stine, was a stay-at-home mother. Stine was Lewis and Anne's firstborn, followed by younger brother Bill, and finally Pamela, the Stine brothers' baby sister. Although the Stines were far from wealthy, they manage to live in a comfortable house on a tree-lined street. "Bexley was a very wealthy community," recalls Stine:

> The Ohio governor's mansion stood two blocks from my house, along with several other enormous mansions. We lived in a tiny little brick house at the edge of town, three doors down from the railroad tracks. I felt self-conscious because my family didn't have as much money as my friends' families. My dad worked very hard. He never stopped working! He and my mom wanted to keep us in this nice community. And they made sure we never felt poor or deprived. But my brother and I still found it hard to fit in to such a rich town. We couldn't afford to drive around in big cars and wear the latest, coolest clothes.[13]

Stine spent his early years listening to suspense stories on the radio but he also had numerous other hobbies. He loved to read, mostly mystery magazines, comic books, and humor magazines—publications his mother didn't want him reading. One day, Stine's mother gave him a dollar and sent him to the local barber for a haircut. When he arrived at the barber shop, he discovered the owner kept many of Stine's favorite magazines in the shop for the customers to read such as *Mad*, *Tales from the Crypt*, and *Vault of Horror*. Stine sat down and read all the magazines, then hopped into the barber's chair for his haircut. Each week after that Stine told his mother he needed a haircut, and then would head to the barber shop for an afternoon of reading pleasure. "I spent just about every Saturday reading in the barber shop," Stine recalls. "Not until I'd read all the way to the inside back cover did I finally climb into the chair for my usual ten-second trim. I spent so much time at the barber shop that the barber started calling me 'son.'"[14]

Meanwhile, Stine put the typewriter he had found in his parents' attic to constant use. He may have been a true fan of horror and suspense, but Stine loved humor even more. Typing with one finger—a style he has never abandoned—9-year-old Stine was soon producing a variety of gag books and humor magazines. "I think *The All New Bob Stine Giggle Book* was my first magazine," he says.

> I still have one copy of this masterpiece. Typed on the old typewriter, it is three by four inches, tiny compared to news-stand magazines. The *Giggle Book* is ten pages thick, but has only five pages of text. For some reason, I didn't type on both sides of the paper. This miniature magazine is filled with jokes and riddles.[15]

Here is a typical joke found within the pages of *The All New Bob Stine Giggle Book*:

> TED: I saw you pushing a bicycle to work.
> NED: I was so late I didn't have time to get on it.[16]

Other single-copy "magazines" produced by Stine during this period included *HAH, for Maniacs Only!*, *From Here to Insanity*, and *Whammy*. All of his magazines were written and typed by Stine alone. He provided all the art work—which he admits wasn't very good. In fact, on the front page of the first edition of *Whammy*, Stine lists himself as editor, assistant editor, assistant-assistant editor, contributing artist, publisher, janitor, and assistant janitor, among other titles. His friends were his readers. Usually, Stine would take the latest edition of one of his magazines to school and pass it around for everybody to read. On one occasion, a teacher caught one of his friends reading an issue of *From Here to Insanity* in class. It didn't help matters that his friend happened to be laughing out loud while concentrating on an article titled "How to Read this Magazine in Class!" when the teacher suddenly snatched it from the boy's hands. The incident resulted in Stine being summoned to the principal's office.

Generally, Stine was a good student in school. He typically earned As and Bs, but since he had more interest in writing his own humor magazines than in concentrating on his school subjects he always seemed to just miss high honors. "I was never very interested in school," Stine says. "I was a lot more interested in my writing."[17]

He played the clarinet but his natural clumsiness kept him out of the high school marching band. "If I marched, I had to concentrate on my feet," he says, "which meant I couldn't think about my music."[18] Stine also wasn't very good at sports. Although he enjoyed softball, when it came to hitting he admits to being an automatic groundout to the shortstop. He tried playing football, but was too thin to excel at the sport and found himself pushed around by the heavier players. He also tried basketball but was a horrible shot and seldom scored a basket. His best sport turned out to be bowling, but he was such a klutz that he once dropped the ball on his foot and broke a toe.

Regardless, none of his failures on the baseball diamond, basketball court, or bowling alley seemed to matter to Stine.

While other boys spent their afternoons at football practice, or fooling around with the engine of a jalopy, or fretting over which girl to invite to the Friday night dance, Stine could always be found bent over his typewriter, conjuring up new gags for his self-published magazines or working on short fiction or even a novel.

When Stine turned 13, he participated in a Jewish ritual known as the bar mitzvah. Jewish boys spend years preparing for their bar mitzvahs by studying Hebrew and learning to lead the congregations of their synagogues in prayer. Jewish girls participate in a similar ritual known as the bat mitzvah. When the day of the bar or bat mitzvah arrives, many parents present their son or daughter with a valuable gift. When Lewis and Anne asked their eldest son what he would like as his bar mitzvah gift, Stine asked for a new typewriter. By the time he was a teenager, writing dominated Stine's life. He says, "When I was in high school, my parents would say, 'Why don't you get a summer job?' and I'd say, 'I can't this summer. I'm writing a novel.' I can't believe I got away with it, but I did. I never worked a day my entire childhood . . . I'd spend the entire summers typing. I hate to think what dreadful stuff I was turning out!"[19]

Certainly, writing didn't take up all his spare time. He did have a social life. Stine joined the school chorus and was active in other school activities, once managing a friend's campaign for senior class president. (His friend lost the election.) He dated some of the girls in Bexley and wrote the senior class skit that was performed shortly before graduation. Still, Stine was committed to his ambition to be a writer and spent most of his free time composing stories on his typewriter. "From the time I was nine," he says, "I've had a single-minded life."[20]

When Stine wasn't writing his own humor magazines, short stories, and novels, he was reading books written by well-established writers. He was a big fan of science fiction authors Isaac Asimov, Ray Bradbury, and Robert Sheckley. One of his favorite books by Sheckley was *Mindswap*, which told of a company that gave people the opportunity to occupy the minds of aliens on another planet. According to Stine, his favorite book of all time is Ray Bradbury's story about a haunted carnival, titled *Something Wicked This Way Comes*. "I grew up in the Midwest, and the story of a Midwestern boy who sneaks out of his house late at night and encounters an evil carnival really gave me chills," he says.[21]

Eventually, his parents bought a television set and Stine became devoted to watching *The Twilight Zone*, the horror-oriented anthology show that dramatized strange tales of suspense and the supernatural. It was not unusual for *The Twilight Zone* stories to end with a twist. In many shows, the ending included a heavy dose of irony and occasionally a spot of humor. *The Twilight Zone* aired from 1957 to 1964. The program was created by Rod Serling, a pioneer in suspense on TV. Serling wrote most of the episodes and also served as the host, opening each program by giving the viewers a brief but eerie hint of what would await them over the next 30 minutes. Stine says:

I couldn't get enough science fiction. That's what brought me back week after week to watch *The Twilight Zone* on TV. Rod Serling's weird, supernatural, half-hour TV show hooked me from the start. Serling introduced each story. He said we were about to be caught in 'the middle ground between light and shadow—between science and superstition.' And his voice was so spooky. I liked the whole look and sound of that show. I still watch reruns today.[22]

Did you know...

R.L. Stine, who continually thinks up new ways to scare his readers, harbors a few fears of his own. For example, he is afraid of jumping into a swimming pool.

Stine says his fear of jumping into water stems back to his boyhood and an experience at summer camp. On the first day of camp, everybody had to take a swimming test. Stine was put into the beginning swimmer group called the Tadpoles. He was determined to move up to the next level and earn his Turtle swimming badge.

Writing in his autobiography, *It Came from Ohio: My Life as a Writer*, Stine says:

> To get a Turtle badge, swimmers had to jump into the pool, swim to the other side, then swim back. We Tadpoles all lined up at the edge of the pool. We would take turns jumping in, one by one.
>
> As I got closer and closer to the front of the line, panic swept over me. I knew I couldn't jump in. I could swim easily from one end of the pool to the other. But the idea of *jumping* into the pool froze me in terror. What was I going to do?

When Stine arrived at the front of the line, he found himself unable to jump into the pool. Amid shouts and taunts from the other Tadpoles, Stine turned and walked away. To this day, he is incapable of jumping into a swimming pool. He says, "My . . . nephews think it's very funny. They're always teasing me and trying to get me to jump. They think it's funny that a horror writer is afraid to jump into a swimming pool."

Stine continued to listen to the radio in addition to watching television. He enjoyed the programs by commentator Jean Shepherd. Shepherd's show originated in New York and was broadcast at midnight—a fact that often led Stine onto a collision course with his parents, who would shout upstairs for him to "Turn off that radio!"[23] Stine appreciated Shepherd's talent as a storyteller. "Shepherd told wonderful, funny stories about his childhood, about his family and friends, and about New York City," says Stine. "I loved the guy's humor. I loved the way he made up stories. And I started dreaming about someday going to New York. I think everyone dreams of faraway places. I know I did. I couldn't imagine living anywhere but New York City."[24]

Stine appreciated the work of other humorists. On the radio, he listened to the comic routines of Bob Elliott and Ray Goulding, who were known to their fans as Bob & Ray. On television, he watched the programs featuring Sid Caesar and Ernie Kovacs, whose zany brand of comedy propelled them into becoming immensely popular stars. He also read books by Max Shulman, a humorist whose best-known work is the novel *The Many Loves of Dobie Gillis*, a comic look at college life in the 1950s. And Stine became a devoted admirer of P.G. Wodehouse, the English author who wrote over 100 novels ridiculing what he felt was snobbish British society.

Stine graduated from high school in 1961 and was accepted at Ohio State University in nearby Columbus. Intent on pursuing a career as a writer, Stine majored in English. The school was only a short bus ride away from his home in Bexley. Stine applied to Ohio State University because he wanted to join the staff of *Sundial*, the school's literary magazine. The magazine had already launched the careers of several noted writers and artists, including James Thurber, a humorist and cartoonist for *The New Yorker* magazine. Thurber wrote for *Sundial* and had been the magazine's editor while he attended Ohio State University from 1916 to 1918. Another *Sundial* contributor was Milton Caniff, an Ohio State University student in the 1930s. Caniff was an artist whose *Steve Canyon* comic strip was carried in hundreds of American newspapers. (Steve Canyon was a U.S. Air Force officer whose adventures often took him on daring missions into enemy territory.)

Soon after arriving on the Ohio State University campus in the fall of 1961, Stine walked through the door of the *Sundial* office and offered his services. He says:

> In college, you go to your classes, and the rest of the day is your own. You can do whatever you want. Some students spend it working part-time. Or studying. I spent all of my spare time at the *Sundial* magazine office. *Sundial* was the main reason I went to Ohio State. Even in high school, I dreamed about writing for that magazine . . . For me, joining the *Sundial* staff was a dream come true.[25]

Indeed, *Sundial* would prove to be a cut above *Eloquent Insanity*, *Uproarious Utopia*, and *Bob Stine Presents*—the names of the self-produced humor magazines he was still churning out on his typewriter at home. Produced monthly, *Sundial* was professionally typeset and printed. It featured photographs as well as drawings by talented artists. As a freshman at Ohio State University, Stine joined the staff as a contributor. Soon, Stine found himself becoming the main contributor to *Sundial*, writing virtually the whole magazine on his own. His college friend and fellow *Sundial* contributor, Joe Arthur, recalls walking into the magazine's office and seeing Stine at work. He says:

I came to the office because I had written an incredibly funny spoof about a space flight. I could hardly wait to give it to the editor.

The editor had other things on his mind. He was in a panic. He said the printing company had moved up the deadline to three o'clock that afternoon.

"Bob, are you going to have that story finished?" the editor wanted to know. The editor was so nervous he had chewed his fingernails completely off. I thought any moment he was going to start on his toes.

Bob just nodded and kept on typing.

I thought the editor was kidding me when he said Bob was writing the *whole* magazine. Turned out he wasn't kidding . . .

With time running out, Bob hammered away on that typewriter.[26]

Unfortunately, *Sundial* was losing money, a fact the university wanted to change. The magazine was supposed to rely on its sales to cover costs. If the magazine didn't sell well, the university was forced to pay the bills. When he began his sophomore year at Ohio State University, Stine applied for the job of *Sundial* editor. At Ohio State University, the university's publications board is charged with selecting the next *Sundial* editor. The board is composed mostly of professors. Stine won an interview with the publications board. He showed the board members samples of his work and promised them that if he took over *Sundial*, he would make it more fun to read and, therefore, enhance its sales. "My goal was to put together a monthly magazine that would give college students a whole lot of laughs," he says. "And the price for all this humor? A mere twenty-five cents!"[27] The publication board accepted Stine's application and he was appointed editor of *Sundial*.

After taking over as editor of *Sundial*, Stine started writing stories under the name of "Jovial Bob Stine." It was his way of creating a comical character who could be featured month after month in the magazine. He also hoped the name would set the tone for *Sundial*—showing that the magazine intended to be lighthearted and full of gags.

Indeed, it didn't take long for *Sundial* to adopt Stine's quirky sense of humor. Soon, the publication was lampooning all manner of college life. "We made fun of just about everything on campus," Stine says:

> The Deans of Men and Women were favorite targets. It was the Dean's job in those days to punish college students who broke the university's rules. They sure had a lot of rules. Among them was a curfew for coeds. That's what college girls were called back in those days. This meant on "school nights" the girls had to be in their dorm rooms by 10:30 P.M. On Saturdays it was 1 A.M. Sometimes, during homecoming weekend, they could stay out until 2 o'clock! There were no rules for guys. The guys could stay out all night if they wanted to. Sound unfair? It was.
>
> *Sundial* made major jokes about this. We pictured the Dean of Women as being totally old fashioned. Which isn't much of a reach since she was. We were trying to be funny. But I like to think we did our small part in the early 1960s to bring about change. Soon after, the unfair rules were dropped.[28]

Under Stine's guidance, *Sundial* started to run photos of attractive female students under the theory that more male students would then buy the magazine. Each month, a different female student was photographed somewhere on campus. Stine called it the "Girl of the Month" feature.

And then, Stine had an idea: What if *Sundial* published photographs of a stunningly beautiful Hollywood starlet, telling the readers that the girl in the pictures was an Ohio State University student named "Pamela Winters." (Stine made up the name using his sister's first name for the fictitious student.) Stine found some photographs of a bikini-clad actress lounging on a beach. *Sundial* published the photos as its Girl of the Month feature. In the caption that ran under one of the photos, "Pamela" invited university students to call her for a date. But that wasn't the end of the gag. The phone number Stine listed in the caption belonged to the office of the Ohio State University Student Senate—the university's student government. On the day that issue of *Sundial* rolled off the presses, the student senate office was flooded with phone calls from male students asking to speak with Pamela.

"We had record-breaking sales that day," Stine says. "Eight thousand copies! And all because of the photos of 'Pamela Winters.' The student senate's phone started ringing. It rang and rang nonstop, day and night."[29]

The story does not end there. After a few days of the relentless telephoning, one of the student senators started answering the calls by identifying herself as Pamela Winters. With each call, "Pamela" agreed to meet the caller for a date, asking him to pick her up at her home in Bexley. Actually, the senator gave them Stine's home address. Soon, Lewis and Anne Stine started answering their front door, finding Ohio State University students in search of Pamela Winters. "My parents were not amused," Stine says. "My sister, Pamela, loved it!"[30]

In his senior year, Stine came up with another gag. He would campaign for student senate president. Certainly, the student senate took campus politics very seriously but Stine had no intentions of running as a serious candidate. In fact, under university rules, he wasn't even qualified to be president. Candidates had to be juniors so that the winner could preside over the senate during his or her senior year. That didn't stop Stine from launching his campaign. In an interview with the *Lantern*, Ohio State University's student newspaper, Stine said: "During the past year, the students of Ohio State have come to expect absolutely *nothing* from the senate. Since I'm graduating this spring and won't be around next year, I feel I'm in a better position than the other candidates to give the students absolutely nothing."[31]

Stine's campaign slogan was "Elect a Clown for President— Jovial Bob."[32] He enlisted *Sundial* staff members to dress up as clowns and hand out his campaign literature around campus. He took out advertisements in the *Lantern* announcing his campaign "appearances," stating that "As a Public Service, Jovial Bob Will Not Speak Tonight in the Delta Gamma (Sorority) House. Enjoy yourselves!"[33]

Students loved Stine's mock candidacy, but the university frowned on the campaign. Because he was a senior, university officials refused to list Stine's name on the ballot. Regardless, Stine still managed to poll 1,163 write-in votes out of nearly 9,000 votes cast in the election. It was quite an accomplishment.

Alas, the mock campaign for student senate president would be the last gag of Stine's college career. In the spring of 1965, Stine accepted his diploma, earning a degree in English. Now, he had to find a job. But what kind of job was available to a sharp-witted former college humor magazine editor? Well, in central Ohio there wasn't much demand for a man of Stine's talents. To find a good writing job, Stine knew he had to move to New York City, where most of America's major book and magazine publishers were headquartered. It would take money to travel, to rent an apartment, and to buy food until he started earning wages.

After graduating from college, R.L. Stine taught for a year in Ohio in order to save up some money. He then headed for New York City—where most of the major book and magazine publishers in the United States are headquartered—to try to make it as a writer. This is a picture of the New York skyline.

At this point in his life, Stine was broke. He did not have enough money to make the move. He took a job as a substitute teacher at a local middle school, planning to work for a year, save his money, and then head for New York.

"I've written a lot of horrifying scenes. But I can't imagine anything more horrifying than facing a new class of students each and every morning," he says. "Everyone knows how kids act up when they have a substitute teacher. It's open season. There's always a kid who claims his name is Pete Moss or Ben Dover or Harry Legg. Some girl who says she's Candy Barr. There are kids who sit in the wrong seat. Kids who don't even come to class."[34]

Soon, the school needed a teacher to take over history classes full time. Stine was drafted, even though he had no love for history. He did try to encourage his students to read, though. In fact, he cut a deal with them: if they behaved Monday through Thursday, Friday would be a "Free Reading Day." On Fridays, the students could bring whatever book or magazine they desired to class and, instead of concentrating on history, they were permitted to read on their own. Some students brought in books, but others brought in comic books, copies of *Mad* magazine, and similar publications that were hardly considered worthy of school time. It was all okay with Mr. Stine. In fact, he often swapped comic books with his students and read them out loud to the class. One day, the principal came in to observe Free Reading Day. It so happened that the principal showed up just as Stine was engrossed in the latest adventure of *Spider-Man*.

"I was on edge, waiting for this no-nonsense principal to say something," says Stine. "He looked at the class, he looked at me. He scowled. Then he turned and stomped out. He never said anything to me about the class. Not ever. He didn't tell me I was doing a terrible job. But he didn't nominate me for Teacher of the Year, either."[35]

Stine's first year as a teacher ended in June 1966. By then he had enough money to make the trip to New York.

He would never look back.

R.L. Stine arrived in the New York City neighborhood of Greenwich Village in 1966. This area around New York University has long been home to writers, artists, actors, and other creative people. At first, Stine struggled to make ends meet—for a time, he survived almost wholly on bologna sandwiches. He eventually landed with Scholastic Incorporated, one of the largest publishers of books and magazines for young people.

3

Jovial Bob Stine

IN NEW YORK City, the neighborhood around Washington Square in Manhattan is known as Greenwich Village. New York University is located in Greenwich Village, giving the neighborhood a lively, college atmosphere. But for decades the "Village" has also been home to writers, artists, actors, and other creative people, who are drawn to the neighborhood because of its permissive, "anything goes" lifestyle.

Many writers have chosen to live in Greenwich Village. Back in the 1920s, some of Greenwich Village's most famous residents were the playwright Eugene O'Neill and John Reed, a radical journalist who wrote about the birth of the Soviet Union. In the 1950s, the so-called "Beat" writers and poets Jack Kerouac, Gregory Corso, and Allen Ginsberg lived in Greenwich Village. The Beats challenged authority. They believed comfortable, suburban lifestyles were boring. They were willing to experiment with drugs. Beat writers were known to spend their evenings in dimly lit coffeehouses, listening to poetry readings and folk singers. The pop star Bob Dylan got his start playing folk music in Greenwich Village coffeehouses.

Stine arrived in Greenwich Village in 1966, taking up residence in a tiny apartment on Waverly Place. He says, "Picture it: New York's Greenwich Village. Narrow streets lined with brick townhouses and apartment buildings. Crowds of artists, poets, writers. Coffeehouses. Bookstores. Bookstores that stayed open *all night!*"[36]

Even though Stine had saved money during his year as a teacher, he still had very little to live on once he arrived in Greenwich Village. For months, Stine survived almost wholly on bologna sandwiches. "There were times when my stomach ached from hunger," he says. "I even considered leaving my apartment and going back to Ohio. But I didn't. I reminded myself I had more important things to do. I needed desperately to find a job."[37]

Stine's first job in the publishing industry was on the staff of *Institutional Investor*, a magazine read by people who manage millions of dollars for pension funds, insurance companies, and similar organizations. Stine didn't know anything about the stock market or investing money; indeed, there would be no opportunity to write gags or funny short stories for *Institutional Investor*. People read *Institutional Investor* to learn how to make money through the stock market. In fact, Stine wasn't even offered a writing job—the publisher needed someone for the production department. Stine's job was to help produce the pages, designing them to display stories and photographs. Stine knew something about production work because he had supervised the design of the pages for *Sundial*. Still, he was hopelessly in over his head and was fired after one day on the job.

He soon found another job. Again, there would be no opportunity to write funny stories, but at least this time Stine would have an opportunity to use his talent as a writer. He found a job with a magazine publisher that produced publications for teenage readers. Mostly, they were fan magazines with names such as *Mod Teen*, *15*, and *Screenplay*. Each magazine featured interviews with television, film, and recording stars. On his first day on the job, the publisher told him to write an interview with Glen Campbell, a major television and recording star.

Stine told the publisher he didn't know much about Campbell, but he would give the story a try. He asked her if she knew how to get in touch with the star. The publisher laughed. "I didn't say *do* an interview," she told Stine. "I said write an interview."[38] She handed Stine a stack of newspaper clippings about Campbell, pointed him toward a typewriter, and told him to get to work. Suddenly, Stine realized what the publisher had in mind: he was to make up the interview.

He says, "In less than an hour I'd written, 'Glen Campbell: Two Men I Call Friend.' It was pure fiction. The article was accepted and it appeared in an issue of the magazine *Country & Western Music*.

"I went on to 'interview' all of the big stars of the 60s—the Beatles, Tom Jones, the Rolling Stones, the Jacksons. Except I never interviewed anyone. *I made up all of my stories.*"[39]

Today, legitimate newspaper, magazine, book, and Internet publishers strive for accuracy and factual reporting. Politicians, stars, and other famous people whose words have been made up by reporters have initiated significant lawsuits and collected millions of dollars in damages. But in the 1960s and before, magazines—particularly publications aimed at teenage audiences—regularly made up their interviews with the stars. And for the most part the stars didn't mind. The publicity helped them sell records and tickets to their movies. "They want all the publicity they can get," Stine's publisher told him. "They don't care what you write about them—as long as you keep writing about them."[40]

Well, it was a writing job and it paid—$100 a week! It was enough money to pay the rent. Suddenly, Stine could afford real food—no more bologna sandwiches. And, what's more, while working for the company he had the opportunity to write horror stories. The company decided to publish a suspense magazine for teens titled *Adventures in Horror*. Stine wrote a tale titled "Bony Fingers from the Grave." The story appeared under the name Robert Lawrence, and was the first of a handful of horror stories he authored for the magazine.

Alas, the job ended too soon. Stine had been on the staff for just a month when the company went out of business. Once again, Stine was out of work. But not for long. He landed next at a magazine titled *Soft Drink Industry*. As the name suggests, it was the trade publication for soft drink manufacturers. It was read by executives in the industry and contained stories about innovations in bottling soft drinks, producing unique cans for soft drinks, developing new flavors for soft drinks, and selling soft drinks to soft drink consumers. "Sound boring to you? It sounded boring to me too," Stine says. "But at least it was a magazine job!"[41]

Stine held the job at *Soft Drink Industry* for more than a year. He found the work tedious and showed little interest in the stories dreamed up by his editors. One time, an editor assigned Stine to write a story about soft drink makers who had started printing advertising messages on their bottle caps. "He held out a bottle cap so I could see the advertising message written inside the cap," Stine says. "I'm sure the editor noticed that I wasn't exactly jumping up and down."[42]

It was during this time that Stine started dating Jane Waldhorn, a young writer who had just graduated from college. Two weeks after they met, Stine and Jane decided to get married. "It was wonderful to be young and on the town in New York," says Stine. "It would be even more wonderful, Jane and I thought, if we could find jobs we liked."[43]

In fact, they would soon marry and begin careers that would set them on their paths toward success in young people's literature. Jane became a successful writer and editor and established her own publishing company, Parachute Press. As for Stine, he would finally reach his breaking point with *Soft Drink Industry*. In December 1968, Stine found a job on the writing staff of *Junior Scholastic* magazine, which is produced by Scholastic Incorporated, one of the largest publishers of books and magazines for young people in the world. Stine says, "I spent the next sixteen years at Scholastic, writing and editing magazines—my life's dream."[44]

Writing for *Junior Scholastic* was nothing like the work Stine had been doing for *Soft Drink Industry* or the teen fan magazines. Now, his job called on him to write

In the early 1980s, R.L. Stine found his writing talents in demand by publishers who wanted him to write adventure novels for young readers. Some of the books he wrote were based on characters from other sources—Indiana Jones of the **Raiders of the Lost Ark** *films, James Bond from the spy film series, and the action figure G.I. Joe. The G.I. Joe books were written under the name Eric Affabee.*

stories for young readers about events and people in the news. The interviews that ran in *Junior Scholastic* were not made up. And the work was fast-paced. Soon, Stine's articles were appearing in other magazines published by Scholastic.

After three years working on *Junior Scholastic*, Stine was asked to take over a new magazine titled *Search*. *Search* was aimed at middle school students who were slow readers. Like *Junior Scholastic*, *Search* was mostly made up of stories about events and people in the news. "It was the first magazine I was the editor of," says Stine. "When I was in school I hated social studies. I had no interest in it. So it was a real challenge for me to be the editor of a social studies magazine! And it was perfect for the readers because they didn't like school and couldn't read well."[45]

Because Stine knew his readers were not dedicated students, he knew he had to present the stories in a form that would grab their attention and make them want to read. So the issues covered by *Search* were presented in a lively, off-the-wall style. For example, for a feature story on medical care, *Search* published a story titled "Medical Care: Is it a Horror Show?" To illustrate the story, Stine used a drawing of a girl in a hospital bed being tended by a werewolf dressed as a doctor. He says:

> It was a very creative magazine . . . We had tremendous mail responses from teachers saying the kids loved it. But it was a little weird for Scholastic. Their other magazines, *Junior Scholastic*, *Senior Scholastic*, were very straight, and here we were doing all these strange things.[46]

Still, his stewardship of *Search* showed that Stine knew how to connect with young people and make them laugh.

His next assignment from Scholastic was to head a new humor magazine for young people titled *Bananas*. Finally, Stine would have the opportunity to edit a humor magazine, fulfilling a dream he harbored since his days back in Bexley when he would sneak off to the barber shop to read the latest edition of *Mad* magazine. Stine says: "It was a happy time for me. All those hundreds of little magazines I had put together in my room when I was in grade school had led to this . . . My own national humor magazine. My life's dream."[47]

Bananas published gags, humorous stories, comic strips, and other features designed to make its young readers laugh. Stories such as "How to Turn Your Uncle Into a Coffee Table" and "How to Tell If You Are an Alien From Outer Space" were published. There was an advice column written by a dog as well as a monthly feature following the antics of a fly named Phil. Mostly, Phil Fly would crack jokes, often at the expense of his girl friend, Phyllis:

> "Gee Phyllis, you're one of the hairiest flies I've ever seen," Phil once told his girlfriend.
>
> "Oh, Phil," she responded. "What a sweet thing to say. Flattery will get you everywhere."[48]

Unlike *Junior Scholastic* or *Search*, there was nothing in *Bananas* that would teach its readers anything about social studies or people in the news. There were no moral lessons for young people hidden between the publication's covers. *Bananas* was intended to be pure fun. Stine says:

> The whole problem with doing humor for children comes from adults. A lot of people seem to think that if a book or

magazine is just funny, it's trash. Adults have their right to read or watch trash. Adults have their right to pick out a book that's just for entertainment, nothing else. But many adults seem to feel that every children's book has to teach them something, has to be uplifting in some way.[49]

As it turned out, Stine found some people in agreement with him. Editors at E.P. Dutton, a New York-based book publisher, found the magazine very humorous and believed Stine could be just as funny between the pages of a book as he was between the pages of his humor magazine. They asked him if he would try writing a children's humor book.

> I spent several weeks thinking up ideas for funny books. And the book I came up with was called *How to Be Funny*. My very first book was a very silly guidebook. I wanted it to be a useful book, one that would help even the most serious kid be funny at the dinner table, at parties, at school, in the principal's office.[50]

Published in 1978, *How to Be Funny: An Extremely-Silly Guidebook*, is essentially 72 pages of jokes, one-liners, humorous riddles, and tips on how to turn even the most boring and routine experiences of life into a gag-fest. What's more, Stine wrote the book under the name "Jovial Bob Stine," the character he had used to brighten up the pages of *Sundial* at Ohio State University.

In a chapter titled "How To Be Funny in School," Stine gives advice on how to enter a classroom:

> As a special favor to the author of this book, Harrison Babble, 13, winner of 17 awards for classroom disruption, has agreed to set down for you here all 10 steps to his world-famous

Clumsy Classroom Clown Entrance. Here is exactly how he performs it, in his own words:

"I wait until they're all in their seats. Then, just as the final bell rings, I step up to the doorway and I (1) bang my head on the door frame, which causes me to (2) drop my books. I (3) bend over to pick up my books and (4) all the change falls out of my shirt pocket. Then (5) leaning down to pick up the change, I (6) rip my pants, (7) stumble over my math book, and (8) break my glasses, causing me to (9) walk into the wall and (10) fall headfirst into the wastebasket."

Of course Babble's 10-step entrance (which he hopes to someday turn into a feature-length movie) will go down in history as one of the great clumsy routines of all time. But as wonderful as it is, many of Babble's classmates wish he wouldn't do it every single morning."[51]

The book also provided tips for readers on how to get laughs at the dinner table (draw eyes on ping-pong balls, then float them in the soup), how to walk funny (bend knees, dip shoulders, cross eyes), how to be funny at parties (fall into the punch bowl), and how to tell a joke.

Always begin by saying, "Stop me if you've heard this one before." If someone says they've heard it, go right on telling it anyway.[52]

He ended the book with a gag bibliography, encouraging his readers to sample other books on how to be funny written by such authors as Tom Foolery, O.B. Sirius, Jerry Germ, Mark Thyme, and Bargil Krilgo, whose book, Jovial Bob told his readers, is "a complete waste of time, very confusing, and not a bit funny. Certainly not worth the $22.95 I paid for it."[53]

Did you know...

R.L. Stine worked as head writer on *Eureeka's Castle*, a puppet show for preschool children that aired on cable television's Nickelodeon network. The show was launched in the fall of 1989 and remained on the air for three seasons before it was canceled, although Nickelodeon continued to show reruns through 1995.

Eureeka's Castle told the story of the magical inhabitants of a windup music box castle, including sorceress-in-training, Eureeka; a klutzy bat named Batly; and Magellan, a lovable dragon. As any fan of *Eureeka's Castle* knows, Batly tended to crash into things whenever he would try to fly. After he picked himself up, Batly would shrug and say, "I meant to do that."

"The personality of Batly, the klutzy bat character, was based on my son, Matt," says Stine in *It Came from Ohio: My Life as a Writer*. "When Matt was a little guy, his hobby was falling down. And every time he fell, he jumped up and cried, 'I *meant* to do that!'"

Eureeka's Castle had many young fans. One time, a young girl visited the set with her mother. When she saw the puppeteers pick up Eureeka, Batly, and the other characters, she burst into tears.

"She thought the characters were real," Stine recalls. "She didn't know they were puppets. I guess that's a compliment."

How To Be Funny earned respectable sales and prompted Stine's publisher to ask him to write more humorous titles. Writing as Jovial Bob Stine, Stine followed up *How To Be Funny* with *The Absurdly Silly Encyclopedia and Flyswatter*, *The Complete Book of Nerds*, *The Pigs' Book of World Records*, *Jovial Bob's Computer Joke Book*, and assorted other volumes of preadolescent humor.

He also found his talents much in demand by publishers who hired him to write adventure novels for young readers. During this period, some of the novels he wrote were based on characters drawn from other sources. He wrote novels about the character Indiana Jones, the popular central figure from the film *Raiders of the Lost Ark* and its sequels, the movie spy James Bond, and the children's action figure G.I. Joe. Sometimes he used pseudonyms. The G.I. Joe books were written under the name Eric Affabee. Another pseudonym he employed was Zachary Blue. Stine also coauthored a number of books with his wife Jane, who by now was the head of Parachute Press. The Stines turned out such books for young people as *Everything You Need to Survive: Brothers and Sisters*; *Everything You Need to Survive: First Dates*; *Everything You Need to Survive: Homework*; *The Sick of Being Sick Book*; and *Bored With Being Bored! How to Beat the Boredom Blahs*.

By now, Stine was a very busy author. He was swamped with requests from publishers to churn out humorous titles for young readers. He soon found himself willing to accept the offers because in 1984, Scholastic cut back on its magazine publishing division and closed *Bananas*. Once again, Stine was out of work. After two years of writing humor books and otherwise working as an author for hire, Stine had lunch with Jean Feiwel, an old friend and editor in Scholastic's book division. At the end of their meal, Feiwel made a suggestion to Stine that would change his life and dramatically alter the direction of children's publishing.

Would he consider writing a horror novel for young readers?

Fear Street was a series of scary books for young readers by R.L. Stine that would eventually include more than 100 titles. In all the books in the series, the characters are drawn into mysterious adventures on Fear Street, where a mansion owned by the sinister Simon Fear burned down amid strange circumstances.

4

From Fear Street to Goosebumps

STINE HAD ALWAYS been a fan of horror fiction, but his experience writing in the genre was limited mostly to the stories he churned out for the teen fan magazine publisher. Now, Jean Feiwel had asked him to write a novel-length story. She did make one recommendation, though, suggesting he name the book *Blind Date*.

It would prove to be all he needed to get started. As his career as a horror writer developed, Stine learned that once he has a title in his head everything else seems to fall into place. He says:

If I can get a title first, then I start getting ideas for it. Like *The Baby-Sitter*. You start to think what's scary about being a baby sitter? Or *The Stepsister*. What would be scary about getting a new stepsister? The title will lead me to an idea about what the book should be.[54]

Stine labored over *Blind Date* for four months. The book tells the story of Kerry Hart, a clumsy high school football player who inadvertently injures his team's star quarterback. Although it was an accident, Kerry gets kicked off the team and is then beaten up by angry teammates. Kerry has other troubles. His mother has walked out on the family, his father is a busy police officer who seems to have little interest in Kerry's life, and his brother Donald is in a mental institution. The reader soon learns that Kerry is harboring his own dark secret.

In the midst of all his woes, Kerry suddenly receives a phone call from a girl named Mandy who introduces herself as Kerry's blind date. Kerry is immediately smitten by the girl, and when he meets Mandy he discovers she is a beautiful blonde. Mandy is perky, smart, and unconventional.

He walked up to her and tried to smile, but his swollen lips wouldn't cooperate. He saw that she had a ribbon in her hair, red and yellow hearts, the kind of ribbon a little girl would wear. Her eyes were pale blue, almost gray. They were translucent. They seemed to be painted on, like a doll's eyes.

Everything about her was light and pale—expect for her lips. Her mouth was wide, pulled up in a wide grin, and she wore dark purple lipstick, which looked even darker and more out of place against her powder-white skin. He thought she looked like Alice in Wonderland, except for those purple lips.[55]

Of course, things start going terribly wrong. Donald breaks out of the mental institution, and Kerry is worried that he is headed home and is possibly homicidal. Mandy reveals she has a dark side and soon leads Kerry to believe she isn't whom she claims to be. Kerry starts receiving threatening phone calls. All the pieces fall together at the end, when Kerry solves the mystery but finds himself enduring painful torture and nearly falling victim to a killer.

Blind Date doesn't have any ghosts, vampires, or other mythical creatures in the story. But there is plenty of suspense and a strong dose of the type of spooky writing that would soon come to make Stine an immensely popular author among young horror fans. Here is how Stine describes Kerry's impressions of Mandy's neighborhood when he arrives to pick her up for their date:

> This neighborhood should look familiar, he thought. He had school friends who lived on Sycamore. He had visited in some of the immense, old houses with their tennis courts, their pools, their room after room of antique furniture you weren't allowed to sit on or play near. But in the dark silence of a cool autumn night, it all looked different. The old houses, carefully shrouded behind tall evergreens and walls of hedges, took on an aura of mystery. Leaves fluttered in the pale light of the street lamps, casting moving shadows that made the smooth lawns seem to churn and bubble as if alive.[56]

Blind Date was published in 1986 under the name R.L. Stine. Stine believed the use of his first two initials in the author's name would add an air of mystery to the book's cover. Much to Stine's surprise, *Blind Date* shot straight to the top of the best-seller lists. The critics weren't particularly kind. *Publishers Weekly*, the main voice of the book publishing industry, complained that the plot of *Blind Date* could be confusing for young readers. However, the magazine praised Stine for moving the story at a quick pace and handling the plot twists with "finesse."[57] *School Library Journal*, a trade magazine for school librarians, said the plot was "complicated and not too believable."[58] And yet, buoyed by the book's strong sales figures, editors at Scholastic asked Stine to author additional novels in the horror and suspense genres. He followed *Blind Date* with *Twisted*, which told the story of a sorority whose members commit murder, and *The Baby-Sitter*, about a teenager who is terrorized while on a baby-sitting job. As with *Blind Date*, both *Twisted* and *The Baby-Sitter* made the best-seller lists. Stine says:

> I began to receive mail from my readers, asking for more scary books. I realized that after twenty-three years of writing, I found something that readers *really liked*. As I read through the fan mail, I began to think: Maybe I should try writing a *series* of scary books. I discussed this with Jane and her partner at Parachute Press, Joan Waricha, and they thought it was a great idea. But we needed a name.
>
> For as long as I've written books, I always start the same way—with a title. If I know the title of the story, coming up with the story itself isn't hard for me.
>
> My new series needed a title.
>
> I grabbed a yellow legal pad from my desk. Rolling my chair over to the window, I prepared to sit there for as long as it took to come up with a title.
>
> As I settled back, the words "Fear Street" popped into my head. I don't know where they came from, how it happened. One moment I was staring out the window. The next moment, I had my title. The words "Fear Street" were repeating in my mind."[59]

And so, one of publishing's most successful series for young readers was born. Eventually, Stine would write more than 100 titles in the Fear Street series for adolescent readers. Stine decided that all the books would be linked by one common element: the characters in each story would be drawn to mystery and adventure on notorious Fear Street, named after sinister Simon Fear, whose mansion burned down amid strange circumstances.

> The street was cursed, people said.
>
> The blackened shell of a burned-out mansion—Simon Fear's old mansion—stood high on the first block of Fear Street, overlooking the cemetery, casting eerie shadows that stretched to the dark, tangled woods. Terrifying howls, half-human, half-animal, hideous cries of pain, were said to float out from the mansion late at night.
>
> People in Shadyside grew up hearing the stories about Fear Street—about people who wandered into the woods there and disappeared forever; about strange creatures that supposedly roamed the Fear Street woods; about mysterious fires that couldn't be put out, and bizarre accidents that couldn't be explained; about vengeful spirits that haunted the old houses and prowled through the trees; about unsolved murders and unexplained mysteries.[60]

The first book in the series was titled *The New Girl*, published in 1989. Shadyside High School gymnast Cory Brooks is showing off in the cafeteria, performing a hand-stand while eating his lunch, when he catches a glimpse of new student Anna Corwin, whom he finds "hauntingly beautiful."[61] The sight of Anna causes Cory to lose his concentration, and he falls head first into a plate of spaghetti. Cory pursues Anna, finding himself bewitched by her beauty. He can't help but fall in love with her, even though

With the success of the Fear Street series, R.L. Stine then embarked on a series of scary books for readers ages 8 to 12 called Goosebumps. Stine said that he wanted readers of the Goosebumps books to feel like they're on a "roller-coaster ride. Lots of thrills. Lots of wild twists and turns." He eventually wrote 87 books in the series.

people keep telling him the girl can't be Anna Corwin because Anna Corwin is dead. Again, Stine keeps the action moving. He puts Cory through numerous tests of courage, sudden plot twists, and heart-stopping jolts of terror. As with *Blind Date, The New Girl* has plenty of suspense but no ghosts or goblins. That would soon change. Eventually, the Fear Street series would include stories of mythical creatures and supernatural powers haunting the teenagers of Shadyside. For example, the series includes a trilogy of stories about Shadyside High School cheerleaders. In *First Evil*, the first book in the trilogy, cheerleader

Corky Corcoran uncovers a century-old evil spirit that terrorizes Shadyside's students.

With the first few books in the Fear Street series, Stine set the tone for the dozens of books that would follow. The main characters would find themselves drawn into mysterious and sinister events in which their lives are placed in danger. The books would also feature adults—sometimes as evil characters, sometimes as helpful parents, teachers, or coaches. Still, in a Stine book the responsibility for figuring out the mystery and dealing with the danger always falls on the shoulders of the teenage protagonists. The violence can be quite graphic at times while at other times the bloodshed is merely suggested. Stine's teenagers do a lot of kissing but their displays of affection never go further. There are social issues aired, to be sure—in both *Blind Date* and *The New Girl*, the theme of mental illness is explored by Stine. And yet, in all the books Stine is careful never to tread too heavily into difficult social terrain, believing that the stories should be regarded as entertainment for his readers. He says, "I don't put in anything that would be too close to their lives. I wouldn't do child abuse, or AIDS, or suicide, or anything that could really touch someone's life like that," he says. "The books are supposed to be just entertainment, that's all they are . . . I believe that kids as well as adults are entitled to books of no socially redeeming value." [62]

His readers' hunger for Fear Street adventures kept Stine chained to his typewriter, churning out manuscripts in the series at the rate of two per month. He would soon find himself much busier. In 1992, Parachute Press editor Joan Waricha suggested that since the Fear Street books were so successful among teenage readers, perhaps preteens would also appreciate Stine's brand of horror fiction. Waricha suggested a series of books for readers ages 8 through 12.

Did you know...

During the 1990s, when R.L. Stine's son Matt was a teenager, he proved to be an invaluable resource for his father. So that his teenage characters would sound like real teenagers, Stine listened very closely to Matt's conversations with his friends. Quoted in the publication, *Something About the Author*, Stine says, "He had lots of friends, and I listened to them. It's very important in these books that the kids sound and look like real kids, suddenly trapped in something horrible."

Stine also read teen-oriented magazines and watched MTV so that he could keep up with music, clothing styles, and other trends popular with teens. Stine says in the *Something About the Author* interview that he is always careful, though, not to use slang. "I'd like these books to be read five years from now, and . . . slang really dates them fast. Besides, most kids talk normal."

Matt would also help inspire his father in other ways. Once, as a young child, Matt had trouble pulling off a Halloween mask. That incident inspired his father to write a Goosebumps book titled *The Haunted Mask*. In another book, *Goodnight Kiss* in the Fear Street series, Stine made his son the main character.

Stine says his son's reaction to all the attention has been, well, annoyance. "Matt never read my books because he knew it would make me crazy," Stine says. "And it worked. It's horrible . . . He'll probably *never* read my books. I've met a lot of authors and none of their kids read their books. It's like a normal way for kids to separate themselves."*

* "R.L. Stine: A Chat with the Best-Selling Children's Author," CNN—Chatpage—Books, *www.cnn.com/COMMUNITY/transcripts/ stine.html*.

"Maybe younger kids would like to be scared too," Waricha suggested. "Maybe you could write a series of scary books that are also funny. You know. Plenty of thrills and chills, without the gore and the blood."[63]

Stine accepted the assignment and again he decided to start with a title. "This time it didn't come easy," he says.

> I thought about titles for the new series day and night. But nothing came to mind. Then one morning I was reading the TV listings in *TV Guide*. (I read them every morning. I get a lot of good ideas for titles in them.) An ad caught my eye. The ad said Channel 11 was running a whole week of scary movies. What really held my attention was the headline in bold type. It read: **It's GOOSEBUMPS Week on Channel 11!**[64]

Stine had his series title.

The first book in the Goosebumps series was titled *Welcome to Dead House*. The book tells the story of Amanda and Josh Benson, whose parents inherit an old house in a far-off town named Dark Falls. Amanda is 12, Josh is 11. The Bensons move to Dark Falls, where strange events start unfolding very quickly.

For starters, their dog Petey runs away as soon as the family arrives at the home. Josh is forced to chase the dog to a nearby cemetery. Next, Amanda thinks she sees strange children in the house—first, a blond-haired boy, then a dark-haired girl. And then, whenever Amanda and Josh do encounter children their own age in the neighborhood, they learn an unusual fact about all of them: everyone claims to have resided in the Bensons' Dark Falls house.

Amanda and Josh finally figure out that they have moved to a town occupied entirely by zombies—members of the living dead. When their parents are captured by the evil spirits, it falls on the two children to find a way to free them. Eventually, they figure out the way to make a zombie go away is to shine a flashlight in his face. The results, Amanda explains, can be quite grotesque:

> Ray moved his arms to shield himself from the light. But I could see what was happening to him. The light had already done its damage.
>
> Ray's skin seemed to be melting. His whole face sagged, then fell, dropping off his skull.
>
> I stared into the circle of white light, unable to look away, as Ray's skin folded and drooped and melted away. As the bone underneath was revealed, his eyeballs rolled out of their sockets and fell silently to the ground.[65]

Stine says he wanted his readers to feel the same sense of excitement while reading a Goosebumps book that they would feel on a "roller-coaster ride. Lots of thrills. Lots of wild twists and turns."[66] Indeed, the Goosebumps books took off like a roller-coaster ride. They would prove to be enormously popular among preteen readers. In 2001, *Publishers Weekly* listed the 565 best-selling children's books of all time. To be included on the list, a book had to sell at least a million copies. The list contained such familiar children's books as *Green Eggs and Ham* by Dr. Seuss, *The Tale of Peter Rabbit* by Beatrix Potter, and the Harry Potter books by J.K. Rowling. No author's name appeared on the list more than R.L. Stine. *Publishers Weekly's* list included 46 titles in the Goosebumps series.

Eventually, Stine would write 87 books in the series as well as some 50 books in a companion series he titled Give Yourself Goosebumps. To keep up with his readers' thirst for new stories, Stine finished a new title every two weeks. Obviously, the techniques he learned at *Junior Scholastic* for writing quickly helped him meet his book deadlines. At the height of the popularity of the Goosebumps and Fear Street series, Stine's books were shipped to bookstores at a rate of 1.25 million copies a month. By 2000, Stine's books had sold some 300 million copies. Indeed, the success of the Goosebumps series earned Stine a mention in the 2000 edition of the *Guinness Book of World Records*. With the Goosebumps books selling a total of 220 million copies worldwide, the *Guinness Book of World Records* declared Goosebumps the best-selling children's book series of all time.

To help sell books, authors often agree to take part in a publicity tour. Typically, an author will travel from city to city, appearing on local radio and television shows to talk about his or her books. Usually, the tour will include visits to local bookstores where the author sits behind a table stacked with books and signs copies for buyers. As the Goosebumps books hit the best-seller lists, Stine found thousands of fans would flock to his book signings. "My biggest crowd was at a mall outside Washington, D.C.," he says.

> We had given out tickets for 500 kids to come. But 7,000 showed up. It was a nightmare, but a thrill. We had to shut off the escalators in the mall so that kids wouldn't get crushed. It was a nightmare! But it was also a thrill for me. I love meeting my readers, but 7,000 is a little too much. I had to send them all home.[67]

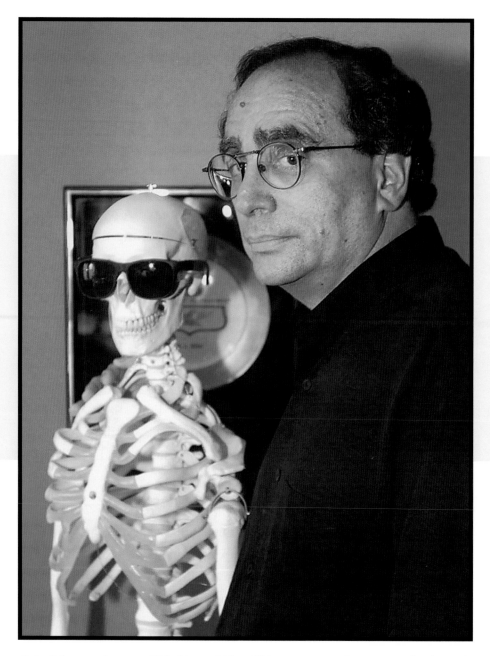

R.L. Stine works out of his Upper West Side apartment in New York City. His office is filled with weird and scary decorations, including a miniature dummy that resembles Stine, phony eyeballs on his desk, and a full-sized skeleton in the corner. These scary, if humorous, items help him write 15 to 20 pages a day.

5

R.L. Stine and the Craft of Writing Horror

THE COMPUTER KEYBOARD that produces the hundreds of thousands of words that make their way into Stine's books lives in an eleventh-floor apartment on the upper west side of Manhattan. It is not a particularly luxurious apartment, given the millions of dollars that Stine has earned through the sales of his best-selling books; nevertheless, it is several cuts above the tiny Greenwich Village flat he occupied after arriving in New York more than three decades ago.

The apartment is lined with custom-made bookshelves, some of which display the dozens of titles Stine has produced over the years. Many of his favorite books line the shelves as well: titles by P.G. Wodehouse, Edgar Allan Poe, Ray Bradbury, and Jean Shepherd, among others. One room in the apartment is devoted to Stine's office. Family photos are displayed in the room, but his office features other, more curious decorations as well: a miniature dummy resembling Stine sits on a shelf; a full-sized skeleton wearing a "Goosebumps" baseball cap dangles in a corner; a few pairs of phony eyeballs sit on his desk. A visitor to his office will also see a phony dagger on display, its eight-inch blade having cut off a plastic finger at the knuckle. The decorations may carry a hint of the macabre but they are far from creepy; instead, they reflect Stine's impish sense of humor. He says, "I knew a writer who wrote scary books, and she had a haunted desk. She had a coffin in the room . . . I can write anywhere. It's the only thing in my life that comes easy to me."[68]

There is nothing funny about his work routine. Stine often labors at his keyboard five or six days a week, starting around 9 o'clock in the morning. Usually, he'll work into the late afternoon. He tries to produce 15 or 20 pages a day, a remarkable output given the fact that during the height of popularity for the Fear Street and Goosebumps books he was churning out novels at the rate of two per month. "I'm very lucky," he says. "I write very quickly, and it usually comes out pretty much the way I want it to, the first time."[69] He claims never to have been afflicted with writer's block—a malady suffered by many writers who get to a point when they simply find themselves out of ideas.

Many times, writer's block occurs when a novelist hasn't planned the story properly. For mystery and horror writers who constantly have to place their characters in danger then find a way to rescue them, writer's block can be a particularly irksome occurrence. Many writers will carry on for dozens of pages, weaving intricate tales, then suddenly find they have placed their characters in a predicament from which they can't be rescued. Stine says that never happens to him. Even at a pace of producing a book every two weeks, he says he still finds the time to carefully outline each story so that before he writes the first word he knows where his characters are going and how he will rescue them from danger. Since he is often under the pressure of deadline, Stine says he typically finds himself writing one book while working on the outline for another. It often takes three of four days to complete an outline. "If I know how it's going to end, then I never have trouble getting there," he says.[70]

When Stine first started writing novels he didn't think he needed to outline all the action beforehand, but soon changed his mind. "I started doing it this way kicking and screaming," he says. "I didn't want any part of these outlines, because sometimes you end up revising the outline, and revising it again until (the editor) approves it, and it's an arduous process. But that's the whole work. An outline helps me see whether or not the books make sense. I always start with the ending—that's the first thing I know. Then I can go back and figure out how to fool the reader, how to keep them from guessing the ending. By the time I sit down to write the book, I really know everything that's going to happen. I can just have fun and write it."[71]

He also never starts a story unless he has already thought of a title. And he spends a lot of time thinking about each character. Stine composes what he calls a "cheat-sheet" for each character that includes information about their personalities, their looks, style of dress, haircut, and the way they speak. "I never get writer's block," he says. "Unlike other writers that start with a story and then make up their title I do the exact opposite, and I have a cheat-sheet for each one of my characters about their personality, the way they look, etc. So there is no possible way that I could have writer's block."[72]

Still, Stine claims he is constantly on the lookout for ideas. He picks them up from all sorts of places. Sometimes, he will get an idea from an article he reads in a magazine or newspaper, or sometimes he is struck by an idea while walking his dog through his Manhattan neighborhood. Sometimes, he will draw on a childhood memory for inspiration.

"I find myself thinking about scary stuff all the time," he says.

> A lot of my ideas for Goosebumps books started a long time ago. When I was a kid, I could never get enough stories. I devoured entire library shelves of fairy tales, Greek myths, Norse legends, and folktales. I loved stories on the radio and TV, too . . . As you might expect, Halloween was my favorite holiday when I was a kid. I always wanted to be something really scary. A ghost. A mummy. A . . . duck? One year, my mother bought me a duck suit. Other kids thought it was pretty funny, but I didn't think it was funny at all. When I wrote *The Haunted Mask* for Goosebumps, I remembered that duck costume and how embarrassing it was. And so I gave Carly Beth, the girl in the book, a duck costume, too.[73]

Sometimes, an idea will pop into his head under the most unusual of circumstances. He says:

> The idea for the Goosebumps book *Stay Out of the Basement* all started with a crazy picture that flashed into my mind. I

imagined a father taking off his baseball cap. Leaves were growing on his head instead of hair. How did the leaves get there? Who is the father? Is he turning into a plant? Is he already a plant?[74]

For the book *Monster Blood*, Stine says:

Those two words just popped into my head. I had no idea what monster blood was. I always liked that title because there is no monster in the book and no blood. Most of my ideas come from getting a title first. I almost always think up a good title and then try to think of a good story to go with the title. One morning a title popped into my head: *Dimwits of Doom*. We will see if I can come up with a story for that one.[75]

And then, he had this idea for the book *Brain Juice*:

One day I was walking down the street and the title *Brain Juice* popped into my head. Then I started to think, what would happen if kids could drink brain juice? Maybe they would get really smart. Maybe they'd get so smart, no one could stand them. It would ruin their lives. That turned out to be one of my favorite Goosebumps books.[76]

Of course, in every book the time comes when Stine has thought of his title, composed his outline, and finished his cheat-sheets. Now, it is time to start writing words. Sometimes, Stine simply sits at his computer keyboard and wades right into the story. He finds he works best when he works quickly, knocking out page after page without worrying how it sounds. He knows he can always go back and revise. In fact, Stine says, he will usually revise the entire book at least once or twice after he finishes the first draft.

If he finds himself unable to think of a way to start the book, Stine says it often helps to tell the story out loud— as if he is reciting the story to a friend over the phone.

Once the book is finished it goes to his editors, who read it and often ask for changes. Stine says it is not unusual for an editor to send the book back with a request to make it scarier. "My editors tell me to make it scarier," he says. "I tend to pull back and they're always saying, 'You have to make it scarier."[77] One time, though, the editors thought he had made the story too scary. He recalls, "*The Girl Who Cried Monster* is about a girl who discovers the librarian is a monster when she sees him eat a kid. The editors thought that was a little too much, so instead I gave him a tray of snails on his desk, and every once in a while he chews one up."[78]

Stine admits that he adheres to a standard set of guidelines when writing a story. For starters, Stine will make sure to keep the story moving quickly. He doesn't spend much time describing a character; indeed, he will dwell little on a character's motivations and weaknesses, often wrapping up those details in a few paragraphs. The characters in Stine's books don't stay in the readers' minds for long after they finish the final page; instead, it is the stories themselves that the readers remember. It is the stories that tempt his fans to come back for more since Stine rarely uses the same characters for more than two or three books.

In Stine's books, the stories generally follow the main characters from beginning to end and rarely branch out into subplots (stories within stories). Depending on what series Stine is working on, the heroes in his books are either teenagers or preteens. Stine likes to have his characters fall into the same age group as his target readers. Usually his characters are ordinary young people who happen to find themselves wrapped up in a mystery or some type of supernatural occurrence. The readers learn that Stine's characters have problems that are typical for young people their age: older sisters enduring bratty little brothers; boys worried about their performances on the gymnastics team; girls developing crushes on boys; boys trying to figure out how to get the girls to notice them; and so on. Once the action starts, their lives will be placed in

Did you know...

R.L. Stine has written more than 400 books for young readers and one book for adult readers. His single novel intended for adults is titled *Superstitious*, which was published in 1995. The story follows college psychology student Sara Morgan, who marries a professor, Liam O'Connor. When gruesome murders start occurring on campus, the clues point toward O'Connor as the killer.

The title is drawn from O'Connor's habit of adhering closely to superstitious rituals, such as throwing salt over his shoulder for good luck and jumping out of the way of black cats.

Stine says he enjoyed writing *Superstitious* but found himself more suited to writing for young readers. In a 1999 interview with CNN, Stine says, "I'm used to writing at a very fast pace. I write a Goosebumps book in about ten days. But my grown-up novel, *Superstitious*, took over four months to write. That was too slow for me. I feel that I can be more imaginative with my kids' books."

danger several times, usually at the end of a chapter. At the beginning of the next chapter, the reader will find out whether the danger was real or just a false alarm. (Mostly, the false alarms come early in the book, while the real danger arrives late in the story.) Stine says his readers "like the fact that there is some kind of jolt at the end of every chapter. They know that if they read to the end of the chapter they're going to have some kind of funny surprise, something scary, something that's going to happen . . . and force them to keep reading."[79] Indeed, false alarms and false clues—known as red herrings—are regular features in Stine's books.

The gore is held to a minimum in the books for younger readers. For the teen readers, though, Stine is known to shower the narrative with buckets of blood. Here is an excerpt from *Goodnight Kiss*, a vampire story in the Fear Street series:

Her fangs lowered, and her face pressed against Todd's throat and she bit deeply.

Deeply.

And drank.

The bat fluttered lower. Lower. But he was too late.

Too late.

The race was lost.

Jessica drank. More and more.

Then, as Todd uttered a loud moan of pain, of helplessness, of ecstasy, Jessica pulled her face back.

The color faded from Todd's eyes as they rolled up into his head.[80]

Certainly, that scene is bloody, but Stine says that's what his readers want in his books. As a horror writer, Stine says,

R.L. Stine lives on the Upper West Side of Manhattan near Central Park. As a prolific author, he is constantly on the lookout for story ideas. He often finds them in newspaper or magazine articles, from a childhood memory, or simply while walking his dog through his Manhattan neighborhood.

his challenge is "to find new cheap thrills"[81] for his readers. "I mean," he says, "disgusting, gross things to put in the book that they'll like: the cat is boiled in the spaghetti, a girl pours honey over a boy and sets ants on him. They like the gross stuff."[82]

Here is an example of a classic Stine gross-out from the Fear Street book titled *First Scream*:

Robin saw his mother's face.

Saw the gray-green bone of her mold-spotted skull.

Saw the black, gaping pits where the eyes had once been.

Saw her hollow, gap-toothed grin. Her jawbone hanging slack. Bits of dried black skin clinging to the hole where her lips had at one time smiled . . . No lips now. No mouth at all. Just rotting chunks of meat and bone . . . He saw the fat brown worm twist its way out of his mother's gaping left nostril.[83]

Despite the abundant amounts of blood and gore, Stine believes the stories are harmless. He thinks he knows how to scare readers, but Stine maintains the scare is momentary and easily forgotten. He says, "Part of the appeal is that they're safe scares," he says. "You're home in your room and reading. The books are not half as scary as the real world."[84]

The one message Stine continually conveys to his readers is that they, too, can write horror fiction if they dedicate themselves to the craft. He urges young writers to use their imaginations and continually search for ways to shock and surprise their readers. For example, he says, it is easy to introduce a dragon into a story, but the challenge to a good writer is to make the dragon a good guy. He adds:

The best stories have the most interesting villains. The more weird and evil your foes are, the more exciting your story will be. It is also much more engaging if a major problem is revealed as the story goes on. Stories become dull if you do not keep experiencing or learning something new.[85]

Stine suggests that young writers should keep journals so they learn how to put their thoughts on paper. They should practice writing their own stories and show their work to other people so they may receive feedback. "Write every day, even if it's just a short journal entry," he says. "Discover what works for you."[86]

He also urges aspiring writers to use simple language that readers can understand easily. "The biggest mistake kids make is using difficult language and sentences that are too long and complicated," he says. "Don't use big words just to use big words."[87]

And, above all, Stine says young writers should read everything they can—not only mystery and horror stories, but other works of fiction as well as nonfiction books. He says there is no telling when an obscure fact a writer may have come across years in the past could one day emerge from his brain and become integral to a plot or character. He says:

> My advice is kind of boring, but I think it's good. It's that you should read, read, read. Don't think about writing things and sending them off to publishers. Publishers really aren't interested in publishing works by kids. The important thing is to read as much as you can. . . . That way, without even realizing it, you build a good vocabulary—and you pick up all different ways of saying things, different styles, different ways to describe the world, to describe people. I don't think anything is as important for someone who wants to be a writer as reading books by many different authors.[88]

R.L. Stine has been soundly criticized because his books contain so much horror and gore, which many feel is inappropriate for younger readers. Horror writers of the past, such as Edgar Allan Poe (1809–1849), also shocked readers with stories and poems such as "The Raven," illustrated here. Critics say that Poe's writing, however, was more thought-provoking and literary than Stine's.

6

Stine Hears
From His Critics

WITH HIS BOOKS selling copies by the millions, Stine soon found his stories falling under the scrutiny of educators, literary critics, sociologists, and others who wondered whether so much horror and gore was healthy for the young minds that were absorbing it all. As such, his stories were studied under the microscope, and it didn't take long for Stine's critics to conclude that they didn't like what they were reading.

One of the first and most heated attacks on Stine's fiction was published in a 1995 issue of *The Weekly Standard*, a news and commentary magazine that has adopted a conservative viewpoint.

The article, which was reprinted in *American Educator*, a magazine read by teachers, was titled, "The Horror of R.L. Stine," and written by fiction writer Diane West.

West raised concerns about whether the genre of what she called "shock fiction" should be read by children as young as 8 years old. She wrote:

> In this literary landscape, narrative exists solely to support a series of shocks occurring at absurdly frequent intervals. Push-button characters serve as disposable inserts to advance the narrative, shock to shock. For example, three pages after "Corky let out a horrified wail when she saw the bright red gush of blood spurting up from Rochelle's neck," we find that "Bobbi had been trapped in the shower room. Somehow, the doors had shut and she'd been locked inside. Then scalding hot water shot out of the showers. Unable to escape, Bobbi had suffocated in the boiling steam. Murdered. Murdered by the evil."[89]

In her criticism, West said she read 30 books in the Fear Street and Goosebumps series, and found their stories strikingly similar. In essence, she said, Stine writes simple stories with no messages or morals and spends little time developing his characters. Instead, she said, the stories are merely vehicles for Stine to throw a shock at his readers every few pages, usually at the end of a chapter. Furthermore, West said, Stine's readers know exactly what they are getting in his books and, therefore, they fully expect the shock when it arrives.

Horror writers of the past, such as Edgar Allan Poe, certainly delivered shocks to their readers, West pointed out, but Poe and the others also offered readers much more than just a fright every three or four pages. Indeed, she said, in many of Poe's stories, such as "The Pit and the Pendulum," "The Tell-Tale Heart," and "Murders in the Rue Morgue," the author wrote thought-provoking stories in which the shocks were often more imagined than real. Many of Poe's stories took the reader to foreign lands during time periods that were hundreds of years in the past, thus offering some-thing of a history lesson to the reader. What's more, Poe also wrote romantic poetry as well as somber verse that many of his young readers, after outgrowing his horror stories, may be prompted to read because they enjoy his work and are ready for a more mature form of literature. In Stine's case, though, West suggested that all his Goosebumps readers could expect after outgrowing Goosebumps were more shocks and more gore in the Fear Street books. She wrote:

> As graphic, horrific, and exciting as Edgar Allan Poe's stories may be, for example, the act of reading them requires a mental engagement with language, with character, with the author's interpretation of events that transforms the action and elevates it above the cheap thrills of a rap sheet. But in shock fiction, a raw catalogue of horrors and grotesqueries is used—not interpreted, not stylized, not in any way transformed by a writer for good or bad—to charge the nerve endings of young readers. In less than deathless . . . prose, shock writers deliver fix after blunt fix to shock (in other words, satisfy) their audience.[90]

Indeed, West insisted that it wasn't just the shocks that bothered her—she admitted that the bloodletting in the Goosebumps series was held to a minimum—but that Stine seemed to have no interest in introducing his readers to a story that involved anything more than having a character simply uncovering something horrible in the attic or basement.

> Childhood and adolescence have been seen as a journey, a passage to adulthood. Moments of truth, phases of growth,

discoveries of a wider world all transform the characters and enrich the readers, young and, in the best works, old. Not so in shock fiction, where there is no journey, and there certainly is no adulthood. Instead, immature characters flail in a stupefying realm of perpetual adolescence where hormonally fraught concerns exist forever out of context. Boyfriends frustrate girlfriends, brothers are unpleasant to their sisters, parents are props, voices scream, blood flows. And nothing ever changes.[91]

She added that Stine's readers are "being encouraged at a critical age to engage in literary pursuits devoid of content, crammed with shock."[92]

West's words were echoed by other critics. Writing in *The New York Times Book Review*, magazine journalist and television critic Ken Tucker said that Stine is "too busy accommodating MTV attention spans to create real personalities" and instead his stories "race from one cheap jolt to the next . . . Most of these books seem to be textbook examples of how not to tell a story. Plowing through an R.L. Stine novel is exhausting because of its endless seesawing rhythm."[93]

Many of Stine's critics are writers and commentators with Christian-based readers and audiences. The California-based Christian author and broadcaster Steven Russo worried that children reared on a steady diet of murder and supernatural stories would become desensitized to violence and, as they grow older, fail to appreciate the real dangers that can be caused by knives, axes, and other instruments of torture and death that Stine employs in his stories.

Goosebumps goes beyond the realm of scary stories that many of today's parents read when they were kids. R.L. Stine's evil-oriented entertainment is filled with ghosts, monsters, witchcraft, sorcery, violence, death and the occult,"

Russo argued. "It would be extreme to say that a young person who reads a Goosebumps book or plays a board game is going to worship the devil and commit a heinous crime. But they will become desensitized to evil and violence. This type of desensitization is subtle and can affect the child long term. Pick up a newspaper or watch the evening news to see just how desensitized to evil and violence the generation of today has become. Goosebumps also has the potential of being a 'gateway' into the world of the occult for some young people. Evil is enticing, and for some kids a hunger for more can easily develop, causing them to search down the wrong path to satisfy their appetite by dabbling in the darkness. This search could eventually lead to more direct involvement with occult practices.[94]

Another critic is novelist Michael O'Brien, author of the Father Elijah series of books that follow the adventures of a Catholic priest on a mission from the Vatican to unmask the devil. "For sheer perversity these tales rival anything that has been published to date," O'Brien said of Stine's books.[95] Richard Arbanes, whose book *Fantasy and Your Family*, attacked several writers of young people's horror and fantasy fiction, including Stine, J.K. Rowling, and J.R.R. Tolkien, wrote: "Stine seems particularly obsessed with murder, especially the killing of young women. Such subject matter becomes all the more disturbing when one views his cover illustrations—they often depict attractive teenage girls in terrifying situations: being stalked, kidnapped or lying dead."[96]

Finally, Stine heard criticisms from other authors of young people's books. In an essay published in *Children's Literature Association Quarterly*, a publication read by school librarians and educators, Canadian Perry Nodelman, an English professor at the University of Winnipeg and author of novels for teenage readers, found much to complain about. For starters, Nodelman criticized the marketing tactics of Stine's publisher, which included in each Goosebumps book an excerpt from the next title in the series. Obviously, Nodelman said, the intent is to draw in the reader and whet his appetite for the next book in the series. Indeed, Nodelman pointed out, the Fear Street and Goosebumps books are numbered so that the young person is not only a reader, but a collector. He said, "Each volume has a number prominently displayed on its spine, and the volumes share the same graphic design, with different titles in the same fonts and different pictures in the same boxes. Like all collectibles, each book looks similar enough to the others to be part of what is clearly a set, but is different enough to make the set incomplete without it."[97]

Nodelman referred in his essay to Stine's book *Attack of the Mutant* in the Goosebumps series. This story tells of a dedicated comic book collector who makes light of a young girl who claims she buys comic books because she enjoys the stories and not necessarily to add them to a collection. However, in the end it is the girl laughing at the collector, for it turns out that she is not a little girl, but an evil alien mutant in disguise. Nodelman wryly pointed out that the true reader in Stine's story wasn't human.

Nodelman also found fault with Stine's decision to write all his stories about white, middle-class, and in all respects ordinary teenagers or preteens, thus leaving no room for minorities or others who may have cause to match wits with werewolves and vampires. What's more, he said, Stine's characters never talk about drugs or sex, and they are never concerned about true-life terror—gang violence or other types of street crime that many children growing up in America have to face everyday.

Most of Stine's characters live in two-parent house-holds, an environment, Nodelman points out, that does not necessarily reflect true life. In addition, Stine never picks a real place as the setting for his stories. His characters do not, for example, live in New York City or Philadelphia or Phoenix or even Bexley, Ohio. Nodelman wrote:

> The families of these children aren't rich, but they enjoy enough material comfort not to need to comment on it. There's a similar lack of detail about the settings, but they

Did you know...

Many of R.L. Stine's books have been adapted for television. In fact, several Goosebumps books were adapted for a television series titled *Goosebumps* that ran for four seasons on the Fox Kids cable television channel.

The series aired from 1995 to 1998, then ran in reruns on the Fox Family and ABC television networks. Some of the most familiar Goosebumps stories were adapted, including *Stay Out of the Basement*, *Welcome to Dead House*, and *Say Cheese and Die!*

Meanwhile, stories in The Nightmare Room series enjoyed a brief run on television. Thirteen of the titles in the series, including *Don't Forget Me*, *Locker 13*, and *Dear Diary, I'm Dead*, were adapted for the series, which aired on the WB television network for a single season from the fall of 2001 to the spring of 2002.

Many theme park visitors have the opportunity to see a production titled *R.L. Stine's Haunted Lighthouse*. The 25-minute 3-D movie, adapted from the 2003 Stine book *Haunted Lighthouse*, plays in theme park theaters. It features real fog and such 3-D effects as rain, splashes of water, and blasts of air. The film stars Christopher Lloyd, Lea Thompson, Michael McKean, and Weird Al Yankovic. The story follows two children, Ashley and Mike, as they meet a salty sailor who leads them on an adventure to a haunted lighthouse.

usually sound like suburbs or small towns. While some books take place during farm or beach vacations, the children never actually live on farms or in urban apartments. Nor do they often live in clearly definable areas with distinctive geographical features of specific regional accents. There's almost no mention of race or ethnicity unless the plot demands it . . . These children seem to be white de-ethnicized mid-Americans, devoid of any consciousness of a specific cultural heritage. And they never express any sort of interest in sex or gangs or drugs.[98]

As the debate over the value of his books raged on, Stine learned that he has as many defenders as critics. Indeed, many journalists, educators, and librarians spoke up in support of Stine. A main argument advanced by his defenders centered on the simple fact that since copies of Stine's books sell by the millions, it is clear that he had sparked an interest in reading among many young people who may have otherwise had no interest in books. Even Diane West was forced to admit that parents supported their children's interest in Stine because it got their noses in books. "I'm thrilled," West reported the mother of one 11-year-old Stine reader saying. "He's literally reading a book a day. He always says, 'Just a few more pages,' when it's time to go to bed. He devours them."[99]

Journalist and author Timothy Harper, who conducted an on-line correspondence with Stine for the Boston-based parenting support group, the Family Education Network, found a lot to admire about Stine's work. Harper wrote:

"Many parents, including my wife and I, had misgivings when Goosebumps started showing up around the house. Sure, they're often funny and usually have happy endings, but

Even though critics decry the level of gore in R.L. Stine's books, he has his staunch defenders as well. Since the books sell in the millions, his defenders argue, Stine's books must be sparking interest among young people who might not otherwise pick up a book.

they're also violent and can be really, really scary for the second-to-sixth graders at whom they're aimed . . . In corresponding with Stine, reading his books, talking to my own grade-schoolers and friends about Goosebumps, and looking in at some of the email between Stine and young fans, I have pretty much overcome my misgivings about his work. Yes, some of it is violent and scary. But Stine does something that most teachers and parents struggle with: He gets kids, especially boys, to read on their own.

Stine's gift is in writing the way kids talk. Awesome. Cool. Totally awesome. Definitely weird. That's probably one reason so many kids love him, and so many teachers and parents have mixed feelings. It ain't literature, they say. Kids should be reading good stuff. But at least Stine gets them reading.[100]

One person who jumped to Stine's defense was Naomi Angier, a young adult librarian for the Multnomah County Library in Portland, Oregon. Angier told a reporter for the magazine *U.S. News & World Report*, "When I was young in the 1960s, I loved Nancy Drew. New York City libraries wouldn't carry the Drew books—they weren't 'good literature.' Besides, if R.L. Stine wasn't writing Goosebumps, many of his readers wouldn't be reading."[101] Angier and other librarians said they are confident that young people starting off on Goosebumps books would eventually move on to much more important literature. Helma Hawkins, youth services coordinator for the Kansas City Public Library in Missouri, told the magazine, "Our slogan is 'equal trash for all.'"[102]

And as to whether the violence in Stine's books helped desensitize his readers, child psychiatrist Leonore Terr dismissed the notion. "Most kids can separate fiction from real life," she told *U.S. News & World Report*.[103]

The most vigorous defender of Stine's fiction is Stine himself. Asked in an on-line interview to respond to his critics, Stine said:

> Well, I think they're totally wrong. I think my books are really healthy, and I think they help kids deal with a lot of anger.
>
> Also, I don't really think mass killers read these books; I've never heard of somebody reading one and then running out and doing something horrible.
>
> And I think violence in movies and on television is very healthy. Everybody has these pent-up feelings, and I think it's good relief to be able to sit and watch it.
>
> People who say kids are going to be influenced don't realize that kids are very smart; it's insulting to kids. Whenever there's some horrible tragedy they start saying, 'Well, let's make sure kids don't go to these movies,' or 'Let's censor the lyrics in their music, and give them a curfew.' Every solution is a punishment, not a solution.
>
> There are a lot of people who don't like young people and resent them. They are the ones who try to solve serious problems by punishing kids.[104]

Despite the support Stine received from writers, librarians, psychiatrists, and others, he continually finds his books challenged by parents and educators who have a lot to say about the type of books that children read and should read. Indeed, as Stine was soon to learn, many bitter feelings would be aired and harsh words exchanged as parents and teachers wrestled over the issue of whether his books belong on the shelves of school libraries and in the hands of young readers.

Controversial books such as R.L. Stine's may even be banned in some school districts. Even though the U.S. Constitution's Bill of Rights guarantees freedom of speech in this country, the United States has a long history of censoring books deemed lewd and unsuitable for the public. Here, police in Boston, Massachusetts, confiscate books in 1919.

7

Censoring Goosebumps

THE CRITICISMS LAUNCHED against Stine by Diane West, Ken Tucker, and other writers and commentators were stinging, to be sure, but in an open society, criticism aired in the realm of public consciousness is welcome and encouraged. Still, when a book is criticized an unfortunate outcome is often a call for its censorship. Sometimes, opponents of a book have succeeded in convincing school and library officials to remove the book from the shelves or otherwise restrict its availability to young readers.

Indeed, each year hundreds of books face censorship fights. Typically, a teacher assigns the book to students or a librarian orders it for the school library's shelves. The book may focus on an issue that some parents or members of the community find objectionable. These people then raise concerns with the school board, which may order the book removed from the classroom or library, or impose rules that strictly limit its availability to students. Often the people who object are very conservative in their lifestyles, and how they want their children to grow up. The most common book themes that are objected to are those surrounding portrayals of religious images or people, images of the devil portrayed in a positive or seductive light, and the use of magic.

Each fall, the American Library Association (ALA) sponsors Banned Books Week to call attention to censorship. In 2003, the association reported that 458 books faced censorship battles. Among the most challenged books were novels in the Harry Potter series, authored by J.K. Rowling—some people objected to the supernatural and magical themes of the series—and the books in the Alice series, written by Phyllis Reynolds Naylor, because of the author's use of offensive language and sexual content. Sometimes, people object to books that are regarded as classics. John Steinbeck's book *Of Mice and Men*, which can be found in middle school and high school English classes throughout America, made the association's list of "Ten Most Challenged Books of 2003" because of the author's use of offensive language. Other classic books that find their way onto censorship lists have included *The Catcher in the Rye* by J.D. Salinger, for its offensive language, *The Adventures of Huckleberry Finn* by Mark Twain, for language that some critics believe is racially insensitive, and *The Color Purple* by Alice Walker, for its sexual content.

Indeed, despite the Bill of Rights, which guarantees freedom of speech, book censorship has a long history in the United States. In colonial times, parents and educators worried whether fairy tales were appropriate reading material for children because magical fairies, giants, and other mythical creatures were contrary to the lessons of the Bible. In the nineteenth century and early twentieth century, parents ripped so-called "dime novels" out of their children's hands. They were worried that the stories of death-defying adventure would lead their children down dangerous paths. "These books, like liquor, work insidiously, damaging in ways that are not always quickly apparent," said Franklin Mathieson, librarian of the Boy Scouts of America, in a 1915 speech.[105] Over the next few decades, many librarians would keep books in the Bobbsey Twins, Nancy Drew, and Hardy Boys series off their shelves, believing the mysteries, which are written for young readers, provided no moral lessons and, therefore, were not suitable for young minds.

Even today, librarians find themselves thinking twice before stocking Stine's books on their shelves. When a box of books donated by a parent arrived at the school library in Westchester Elementary School in Kirkwood, Missouri, school librarian Pamela Strang opened the box to find an assortment of Goosebumps books on top. After hesitating, Strang reluctantly placed the Goosebumps books on the shelves. "I'm not into censoring," she told a reporter. "But I think there's a lot more out there for children than shock fiction . . . I thought about it. And I decided, 'Why not?' The books are age appropriate. I don't know if they are quality literature, but they are popular. They are recreational reading. That's it."[106]

R.L. Stine's books did not make the American Library Association's "Ten Most Challenged" list for 2003. In fact, the American Library Association reported that in 2003, for the first time in years, the Goosebumps and Fear Street books had dropped off the list of most censored books. "Off the list this year, but on the list for several years past, are the Goosebumps and Fear Street series, by R.L. Stine, which were challenged for being too frightening for young people and depicting occult or 'Satanic' themes," the ALA reported.[107]

Still, Stine has endured his share of censorship fights. In the fall of 2004, the American Civil Liberties Union placed the Goosebumps series in sixteenth place on its list of the 100 most frequently challenged books in the decade from 1990 to 2000. A typical challenge to Stine's books surfaced in 2003 in Georgia, when the Crawford County School Board withdrew the Fear Street book *Double Date* from the middle school library shelves. *Double Date* tells the story of a school Romeo named Bobby who decides to date the Wade twins, Samantha and Bree, behind each other's backs. Soon, Bobby gets the idea that one of the twins is trying to kill him but he doesn't know which one.

The story alarmed Crawford County parent Katie Jones, who convinced the school board to remove it from the library. Crawford County School Board's decision sparked Beverley Becker, associate director of the American Library Association's Office for Intellectual Freedom, to tell a Georgia newspaper, "The role of the library is to provide access to information across a spectrum of ideas so people can choose for themselves. The crux of the issue is, who will decide who has access to materials? It gets into the issue of censorship."[108] Still, *Double Date* was withdrawn from the shelves in Crawford County. Similarly, in Gainesville, Florida, the Stine book *Fall Into Darkness* was restricted to readers in the eighth grade and above.

The battles for freedom of speech versus censorship continue to this day and R.L. Stine has endured his share of censorship fights. The American Civil Liberties Union placed the Goosebumps series in sixteenth place on its list of 100 most frequently challenged books in the 1990s.

In most cases, though Stine's books have prompted parents to call for their removal, the books have managed to remain on the library shelves after a public airing of the issue. School board members and library officials have had to weigh the desires of parents in their communities to protect their children from what they regard as inappropriate literature against an author's right of free speech that is protected by the U.S. Constitution. In Panama City, Florida, for example, parents Lisa and Kip Clinton asked the Bay County School Board in 1996 to remove 43 copies of the Goosebumps series from the county's elementary schools. Lisa Clinton told a news reporter that she first learned of the Goosebumps books when her daughter, a third-grade student, told her that her teacher had read *Night of the Living Dummy II* to the class. "We're very cautious as to what our children view," Clinton told the newspaper. "We believe in letting children be children, but not to the point of showing them all the evils in the world."[109]

In their letter to the school board, the Clintons insisted that *Night of the Living Dummy II* should be banned from the schools because of its depictions of violence, vandalism, and evil chants. Their formal request to the school board included four other Stine books—*The Barking Ghost, The Haunted Mask, The Scarecrow Walks at Midnight,* and *Say Cheese and Die!*—which the Clintons said contained references to Satanism, demonic possession, and numerous acts of violence. The letter to the school board stated: "These books do absolutely nothing to edify our children, or to promote descent [sic] morals, or kindness to one another. They are another tool to demoralize our precious children. It is obvious of the author's mentality towards our children."[110]

The Clintons weren't the only Bay County residents who found the Goosebumps books objectionable. Sarah Hollingsworth said she found herself offended while reading a Goosebumps book about a werewolf to her 11-year-old granddaughter. "I always thought God's Word was the only one to inspire, but I found out different," Hollingsworth told the school board. "(Satan) is taking these books and entering into a child's mind."[111] But another Bay County parent, Lisa Hanson, suggested that if the school board bans Goosebumps books, what would it do if a parent asks that a story such as *Romeo and Juliet* be banned? "Everyone can find something offensive and detrimental in everything they read," Hanson told the school board. "Where will it stop?"[112]

The request by the Clintons sparked a debate in the community of Panama City while the school board spent several months deciding whether to pull the Goosebumps books out of Bay County classrooms and libraries. "On the face of it, these books are inoffensive. I don't see how any reasonable people could read these and be offended," insisted Gloria Pipkin, a former Bay County English teacher and member of the Florida Coalition Against Censorship.

> I've always maintained that even a child who finds material uncomfortable, objectionable or offensive should be allowed to determine if it's inappropriate and should be given alternative materials. That's written into the policy that governs the review of instructional materials. But where I draw the line is where a parent is wanting to control not only her own child's reading but the reading of every child in Bay County.[113]

And Craig Bush, the principal at the Panama City school where the Clintons' daughter attended, said, "These books aren't personally offensive to me. My daughter has some. She's read some. The parents have raised an issue, and there's a very good process to review it."[114]

Again, Stine's defenders offered the argument that the author is responsible for turning millions of young people on to reading. Cynthia Maloney, director of Book Club marketing for Goosebumps publisher, Scholastic Incorporated, said that her company receives some 1,000 letters a week from Stine's readers and their parents. Most of the letters are positive, she said. "We hear, 'My child never read a book but is reading now, thanks to R.L. Stine,'" she said.

> What's really heartwarming are the (letters from) kids who are learning-delayed, and they want desperately to read the books and be a part of the phenomenon . . . The one thing to keep in mind is you have children reading at a time when

today's world is all TV or video games, all 'received' information and passive. Reading is work. It's hard work. It's your own imagination creating the images.[115]

As for Stine, he has continually reiterated his feeling that his readers know what's best for them. "I think that kids are really smart," he said in an on-line interview, "and I don't think they will read anything that is inappropriate for them."[116]

After mulling over the Clintons' request for some two months, the Bay County School Board decided to keep the Goosebumps books on the shelves of the elementary schools, although the board adopted a policy giving parents the right

---

Did you know...

With more than 300 million copies sold, it would seem that every book that R.L. Stine has written has been a success. That is not true. Just before launching the enormously successful Goosebumps series, Stine authored three humorous science fiction books that were part of a series he called Space Cadets.

The books, which were published in 1991 and 1992, are titled *Jerks in Training*, *Bozos on Patrol*, and *Losers in Space*. Stine loved writing the books, but readers mostly ignored the stories.

In an interview Stine says, "I did a book series before Goosebumps that I loved. I always wanted to write funny stuff, and I did a series called Space Cadets about the five dumbest cadets in the Space Academy. It was just slapstick humor. I loved these books; they were my favorites. I thought they were really funny. No one bought them, they were a total flop."*

* Teen Ink "Interview with Author R.L. Stine," Interview: Author, R.L. Stine, *http://teenink.com/Past/2001/June/Interviews/RLStine.html*.

to have a substitute book made available to their children if they find the contents of the story objectionable. In voting to keep Stine's books in the elementary schools, School Board Member Henrietta Swilley dismissed the notion that Goosebumps books desensitize children to violence and prompt them to imitate the acts depicted in the books. She said, "Most of us have studied all kinds of literature, but did not go out and imitate it. Otherwise, we'd go out and imitate the (old woman who lived in the shoe) who had so many children she didn't know what to do, so she whipped them all soundly—that would be child abuse today."[117]

In Minnesota, the Anoka-Hennepin School District also wrestled with banning Stine's books from its elementary schools in 1996 and 1997. The Anoka-Hennepin district's debate over the books drew national attention when the cable television network C-SPAN televised a public hearing held to determine whether residents supported the ban on Stine's books. Ultimately, the school district elected to keep the Goosebumps books on the shelves. "Students have the right to choose their own reading materials," said a school district committee that examined the controversy. "The responsibility for good decision making regarding reading choices should rest between an individual child and their parents."[118] That decision was applauded by Anoka-Hennepin parent Sharon Cuskey, who said, "The small group of parents supporting this ban-the-book movement need to be reminded that it is their parental responsibility to censor what their children listen to, watch, and read, and not their right to decide what is appropriate or acceptable for my children or any other children in the school district. Before you decide whether or not to fire up the furnace and ban these books, please remember the real issue that lies below the surface, and that being freedom."[119]

In 2003, R.L. Stine (left) and other authors traveled to Moscow with First Lady Laura Bush (right) to promote a love of reading to Russian children. The First Lady is a former librarian and reading teacher who feels strongly about promoting literacy.

The Nightmare Room . . . And Beyond!

BY THE LATE 1990s, Stine had weathered the attacks by his critics. His books remained widely available to young readers, despite the constant censorship battles. He now found himself eager to take his horror fiction in a new direction. Stine still intended to write for young readers, but now sought to introduce a more suspenseful brand of horror. He envisioned a series of books that would rely less on shock and more on plot: in the new series, the terror would be introduced slowly then gradually increase until it finally overwhelmed the characters near the story's conclusion. In 2000, Stine's book *Don't Forget*

Me, the first in The Nightmare Room series, was introduced to readers.

He says, "Goosebumps was like a wild roller coaster ride—there were monsters and scary things at every corner, jumping out to get them. But The Nightmare Room is more like a fun house. It's a little quieter. It's more like walking into a room where everything seems normal, but suddenly the room starts twisting or the walls start closing in on you."[120]

As a boy growing up in Ohio, Stine was a big fan of the television show *The Twilight Zone*. He recalled how the host, Rod Serling, would briefly address the audience at the start of the show, giving them a short summary of what was to come next and leaving them with just a hint of an idea of the terror that was about to unfold. Stine decided to start each of The Nightmare Room books with a brief, Serling-like introduction. He begins *Don't Forget Me* with these words:

> For all of us there's a place where true horror waits—our own personal Nightmare Room. You might find it anywhere—at home, at school, in the woods, at the mall . . . in your MIND. Take one step, shut your eyes—and you're there. You've crossed the line. You've crossed over, from reality to nightmare.
>
> I'm R.L. Stine. Let me introduce you to Danielle Warner. She's that worried-looking girl with the solemn, dark eyes . . .[121]

As the story unfolds, the reader learns that Danielle and her little brother Peter have just moved into a new home. Danielle soon starts hearing voices coming from the basement. It turns out that the voices belong to the "forgotten ones," the prior residents of their home, which Danielle learns is known around town as the "Forget-Me House." It seems that everyone who lives in the Forget-Me House loses all memory of family and friends. What's more, everyone else—parents, friends, teachers—lose memory of the forgotten ones. The story follows Danielle as she tries to save Peter, as well as herself, from joining the forgotten ones.

Don't Forget Me includes a few plot twists. For example, early in the book Stine introduces the notion that Peter starts forgetting things because he has been hypnotized by Danielle and her friend Addie, who have been rehearsing a mock hypnosis act for a school talent show. When Peter volunteers to let Danielle and Addie practice their lines on him, the two girls conclude that they really did hypnotize Peter. And so, Danielle spends a considerable part of the story trying to figure out how to snap Peter out of his hypnotic trance while ignoring the clues that suggest a supernatural force has taken over the house. Danielle tells Addie:

> "I remember it so clearly. You said, 'It's not funny. Forget about it. Enough already.' That's what you said, Addie. '*Forget about it!*'"
>
> Her green eyes flashed. "So? So what?"
>
> "Well—that's what he did!" I screeched. "He forgot about it. He—he listened to you, Addie. And when he woke up, he forgot just about everything!" [122]

As Danielle eventually discovers, Peter was never under hypnosis and was, instead, a victim of the evil curse that possesses the occupants of the house. Many of the familiar Stine elements are present in the story. Danielle tends to think her brother is a pest. She also has a king-sized crush on Zack, who only starts taking an interest in her after Peter begins to forget things. Of course, Danielle's parents aren't home—they have taken a business trip, leaving Danielle to struggle through the terror on her own. And, finally, there is a happy ending. Danielle figures out a way to defeat the forgotten ones and break the curse on the house. Or does she? At the end of the book, Stine leaves the issue in doubt.

Stine says:

> You know, I wrote 87 Goosebumps books. And I thought it was getting a little harder to come up with the stories. I needed a different focus. It was time for a change. But they're still the same kind of stories, though—good, creepy fantasies.[123]

Stine has written 15 titles in The Nightmare Room series. Other titles include *Locker 13*, in which a high school student named Luke discovers on the first day of school he has been assigned a new locker with a decidedly unlucky number; *Dear Diary, I'm Dead*, in which Alex Smith discovers entries writing themselves into his diary; and *Liar Liar*, which tells the story of a habitual liar named Ross who manages to lie himself into a whole new reality.

The early years of the 2000 decade were busy ones for Stine. For starters, he maintained a hectic writing schedule and also found time to become an international ambassador for literacy. In 2003, Stine traveled to Moscow with First Lady Laura Bush on a mission to spread a message supporting the love of reading to Russian children. Literacy has always been an important issue to the first lady, who once worked as a librarian and reading teacher in a Texas elementary school. Other authors who made the trip with Bush were Marc Brown, the author of the Arthur series for beginning readers, and Peter Lerangis, one of the contributing authors to the Baby-Sitters Club series of books.

In Moscow, the three authors attended a book festival chaired by Lyudmila Putina, the first lady of Russia. Bush says she invited Stine and Lerangis to make the trip because their books have been translated into Russian.

During his appearance at the Moscow book festival, Stine sat surrounded by his young Russian fans and, with their

Did you know...

R.L. Stine has some personal favorites among the more than 400 books that he has written. Two of his favorite stories were not written in the horror genre. They include *Phone Calls*, which was published in 1999, and *How I Broke Up With Ernie*, published in 1990.

Phone Calls is a humorous story that unfolds around a series of telephone calls made by teenagers Diane and Julie, who start out as friends but soon find themselves plotting and scheming to embarrass and humiliate each other. *How I Broke Up With Ernie* is a romance that follows Amy as she tries to break up with a guy everybody thinks is perfect.

As for his scary stories, Stine counts the Goosebumps book *Brain Juice*, published in 2000, among his favorites. Most of the Goosebumps books are told from the viewpoint of the young protagonists. *Brain Juice*, however, unfolds through the eyes of Morggul and Gobbul, a couple of aliens who plan to kidnap Earthlings and take them back to their home planet as slaves. Meanwhile, the two young heroes, Nathan and Micah, drink an elixir concocted by the aliens, believing the "brain juice" will make them supersmart.

In an interview Stine said, "There's a funny novel I wrote called *Phone Calls* that is about teenagers calling each other. It's really funny, very twisted. There's another funny one, *How I Broke Up With Ernie*. I'm really proud of those. And there are a couple of Goosebumps I'm really proud of; *Brain Juice* is a perfect combination of scary and funny, I think."*

* Teen Ink "Interview with Author R.L. Stine," Interview: Author, R.L. Stine, *http://teenink.com/Past/2001/June/Interviews/RLStine.html*.

help, worked out the details for a new story about a boy and a haunted car. When Stine's part of the program concluded, Bush told the crowd, "A really good book makes you feel like you are part of the story."[124]

After returning from his mission to spread literacy in Russia, Stine was invited to take part in a similar program in the United States. Stine was one of more than 70 authors and poets who participated in the Library of Congress National Book Festival in Washington in the fall of 2004. Stine was among 10 children's authors asked to speak at the festival. In addition to the children's authors, the festival included some of the literary community's most esteemed writers—including novelist Joyce Carol Oates, biographer and historian Douglas Brinkley, science fiction writer Ben Bova, and mystery writer Lawrence Block. Certainly, by including the name of R.L. Stine on the list, the organizers of the event left little doubt that Stine's value as a writer is appreciated and admired.

The National Book Festival was staged on the National Mall in Washington and hosted by Laura Bush. Some 70,000 people attended the festival, where they took part in seminars, talks by authors, and book-signings.

Meanwhile, Stine found the time to plan and write books in two new series. In 2003, *Dangerous Girls*, the first book in a series of the same name, appeared in the bookstores. The Dangerous Girls books are aimed at an older teen audience; indeed, the first book in the series spans 256 pages. The books tell the story of twin sisters Destiny and Livvy Weller, who return home from summer camp and discover they are vampires. Destiny struggles to free herself and her sister from the curse, but Livvy wants to test her new dark powers. The second title in the series, *The Taste of Night*, was released in 2004. The book follows

In the late 1990s, R.L. Stine introduced a new series of scary books, the Nightmare Room series. These books rely more on plot and less on shocks, so that the terror gradually builds to the story's dramatic conclusion. Titles in the series include Don't Forget Me, Locker 13, *and* Liar, Liar.

Livvy and Ross, Destiny's old boyfriend who Livvy has turned into a vampire. Together, Ross and Livvy prey on other teens.

In the fall of 2004, another new series from Stine premiered. Titled Mostly Ghostly, the series is aimed at readers between the ages of 7 and 10. Unlike Goosebumps, Fear Street, and the Nightmare Room, the Mostly Ghostly books are planned to follow the same characters from book to book. The first book, titled *Who Let the Ghosts Out?*, introduces Stine's readers to the characters and establishes their story: a couple of kids named Nicky and Tara Roland discover they are ghosts. They are shocked to find the Doyle family living in their home, and that the little brother in the family, Max, is a nerd who allows his older brother to push him around. Nicky and Tara need Max's help to learn the truth behind why they are ghosts and what happened to their parents. In return, Nicky and Tara help Max deal with the bullies in his life. Meanwhile, an evil spirit named Phears makes his appearance, surprising Max while he walks his dog Buster:

> As I stared in shock, his mouth opened wider. His black lips pulled back until I could see all his teeth. The lips pulled back farther. The mouth pulled open even wider.
>
> "Buster—?"
>
> I gasped in horror as the lips pulled back . . . back . . . until Buster's whole head disappeared. Was he *swallowing* himself?
>
> His eyes disappeared inside his skin. The gaping mouth slid back over Buster's body. I could see glistening wet, pink flesh—the insides of his throat.
>
> And then, as the fur peeled back, I saw pale bones and gleaming yellow and red organs. Buster's purple, pulsing heart. His rib cage. His balloonlike stomach. His twisting yellow guts.[125]

Phears has turned Buster inside out. He confronts Max, demanding to know where he can find Nicky and Tara. At this point in the story, though, neither Nicky nor Tara have introduced themselves to Max. Max doesn't know who Phears is referring to, so he doesn't tell him anything. Phears promises to return and vanishes—but not before putting Buster back together. Soon, Max does meet Nicky and Tara and agrees to help them discover the truth about how they died, what happened to their parents, and what the evil Phears may have had to do with it all. Soon after *Who Let the Ghosts Out?* was released, the second book in the Mostly Ghostly series, *Have You Met My Ghoulfriend?*, was distributed by the publisher. Four more volumes in the series are due out in 2005.

Who Let the Ghosts Out? and *Have You Met My Ghoulfriend?* earned decent reviews when they were released just before Halloween in 2004. *The Washington Post* said:

> These books are pretty scary. *Who Let the Ghosts Out?* starts with a brother and sister walking home alone on a dark October night and discovering bit by bit that every person and thing they know has disappeared. Then there's a downright gross scene in which Buster, the family dog, turns himself inside out while he's on a poop break. While having ghosts living in your room isn't typical for a 12-year-old kid, some of the other problems Max faces may be familiar to you. So, go ahead and check out Stine's latest fright-fest. But we wouldn't blame you if you left the lights on long after you've stopped reading for the night.[126]

Many of the young readers who discovered Stine in the early 1990s and became devoted fans of the Goosebumps and Fear Street series have now grown up and will soon be starting their own families. Their children will surely one day want to make their own decisions about what type of books they want to read. Some of them will want a good fright. If they are lucky, their mothers and fathers have kept their old Goosebumps books. Indeed, they may be stored in a cardboard box in the attic, and one day mom and dad will be traipsing up the attic stairs to haul the box down for their children, who will surely devour the contents.

And if, when they find themselves in the attic, they discover a mirror that turns them invisible, well, thanks to R.L. Stine they'll know what to do.

1 R.L. Stine and Joe Arthur, *It Came from Ohio! My Life as a Writer* (New York: Scholastic Inc., 1997), 2.

2 Ibid.

3 Ibid., 4–5.

4 Quoted in Diane Telgen, ed. "R.L. Stine," *Something About the Author* vol. 76 (Detroit, MI: Gale Group, 1994), 222.

5 Stine and Arthur, *It Came from Ohio! My Life as a Writer*, 7.

6 Ibid., 8–9.

7 Ibid., 9.

8 Ibid., 10.

9 R.L. Stine, *Piano Lessons Can Be Murder* (New York: Scholastic Inc., 1993), 6.

10 R.L. Stine, *Let's Get Invisible* (New York: Scholastic Inc.,1993), 35.

11 Stine and Arthur, *It Came from Ohio! My Life as a Writer*, 16.

12 Ibid., 17.

13 Ibid., 42–43.

14 Ibid., 19.

15 Ibid.

16 Ibid.

17 Ibid., 30.

18 Ibid., 34.

19 Quoted in Jim Roginski, *Behind the Covers: Interviews with Authors and Illustrators of Books for Children and Young Adults* (Littleton, CO: Libraries Unlimited, 1985), 207.

20 Ibid.

21 Quoted in "An Interview With the World's Best-Selling Children's Author, R.L. Stine," R.L. Stine—HarperChildrens, *www.harpe childrens.com/catalog/author_inte rview_xml.asp?authorid=14471.*

22 Stine and Arthur, *It Came from Ohio: My Life as a Writer*, 47.

23 Ibid., 8.

24 Ibid., 7–8.

25 Ibid., 51–53.

26 Ibid., introduction.

27 Ibid., 53–55.

28 Ibid., 55.

29 Ibid., 57.

30 Ibid.

31 Ibid., 59–60.

32 Ibid., 60.

33 Ibid.

34 Ibid., 64.

35 Ibid., 66.

36 Stine and Arthur, *It Came from Ohio: My Life as a Writer*, 70.

37 Ibid., 71.

38 Ibid., 74.

39 Ibid., 75.

40 Ibid.

41 Ibid., 77.

42 Ibid., 81.

43 Ibid., 80.

44 Ibid., 83.

45 Roginski, *Behind the Covers: Interviews with Authors and Illustrators of Books for Children and Young Adults*, 208.

46 Ibid.

47 Stine and Arthur, *It Came from Ohio: My Life as a Writer*, 86.

48 Ibid., 85.

49 Roginski, *Behind the Covers: Interviews with Authors and Illustrators of Books for Children and Young Adults*, 209.

50 Stine and Arthur, *It Came from Ohio: My Life as a Writer*, 89–90.

51 Jovial Bob Stine, *How To Be Funny: An Extremely-Silly Guidebook* (New York: Scholastic Inc., 1978), 15.

52 Ibid., 53.

53 Ibid., 72.

54 Quoted in Patrick Jones, *What's So Scary About R.L. Stine?* (Lanham, MD: Scarecrow Press, 1998), 42.

55 R.L. Stine, *Blind Date* (New York: Scholastic Inc., 1986), 68–69.

56 Ibid., 33.

57 Quoted in "Blind Date," *Publishers Weekly*, August 22, 1986.

58 Quoted in Jones, *What's So Scary About R.L. Stine?*, 58.

59 Stine and Arthur, *It Came From Ohio: My Life as a Writer*, 110.

60 R.L. Stine, *The New Girl* (New York: Scholastic Inc., 1989), 18–19.

61 Ibid., 8.

62 Quoted in Scot Peacock, ed. "R.L. Stine," *Contemporary Authors New Revision Series* vol. 109 (Farmington Hills, MI: Gale Group, 2002), 383.

63 Stine and Arthur, *It Came From Ohio: My Life as a Writer*, 114.

64 Ibid.

65 R.L. Stine, *Welcome to Dead House* (New York: Scholastic Inc., 1992), 96–97.

66 Stine and Arthur, *It Came From Ohio: My Life as a Writer*, 114.

67 Quoted in "R.L. Stine: A Chat with the Best-Selling Children's Author," CNN—Chatpage—Books, *www.cnn.com/COMMUNITY/ transcripts/stine.html*.

68 Quoted in Scott Moore, "Plenty of Skeletons in R.L. Stine's Closet," *Los Angeles Times*, October 30, 2000, 3.

69 Quoted in "R.L. Stine," Team 10, Literature, *www.cognivision.com/ timecapsule61/timecapsule61/tea m_10_literature.htm*.

70 Quoted in Laura Deutsch, "R.L. Stine on Why Writing Doesn't Have to be Scary," *Writing*, September 2004, 8.

71 Quoted in Scot Peacock, ed. "R.L. Stine," *Something About the Author* vol. 129 (Farmington Hills, MI: Gale Group, 2002), 185.

72 Quoted in Tracy Rodrigues, "Meeting the Man Behind the Nightmare Room," Time for Kids | Specials, *www.timeforkids.com/ TFK/specials/white/0,6406,17652 0,00.html*.

73 Quoted in "Where Do You Get Your Ideas," Creature Feature— "Where Do You Get Your Ideas?", *www.scholastic.com/goosebumps/ books/stine/ideas.htm*.

74 Ibid.

75 Quoted in "R.L. Stine," Team 10, Literature.

76 Quoted on Teen Ink "Interview with Author R.L. Stine," Interview: Author, R.L. Stine, *http://teenink.com/Past/2001/ June/Interviews/RLStine.html.*

77 Ibid.

78 Ibid.

79 Quoted in Scot Peacock, ed. "R.L. Stine," *Something About the Author* vol. 129, 184.

80 Quoted in Jones, *What's So Scary About R.L. Stine?*, 113.

81 Quoted in Paul Gray, "Carnage: An Open Book," *Time* vol. 142, no. 5, Aug. 2, 1993, 54.

82 Ibid.

83 Quoted in Jones, *What's So Scary About R.L. Stine?*, 131.

84 Quoted in Gray, "Carnage: An Open Book," 54.

85 R.L. Stine, "How to Write Your Own Give Yourself Goosebumps Books," Creature Feature, *www.scholastic.com/goosebumps/ books/stine/writeown.htm.*

86 Quoted in Deutsch, "R.L. Stine on Why Writing Doesn't Have to be Scary," 8.

87 Ibid.

88 Stine and Arthur. *It Came From Ohio: My Life as a Writer*, 140.

89 Diana West, "The Horror of R.L. Stine," *American Educator* vol. 19, no. 3, Fall 1995, 39.

90 Ibid., 40.

91 Ibid., 41.

92 Ibid.

93 Quoted in Jones, *What's So Scary About R.L. Stine?*, 194–195.

94 Steve Russo, "Goosebumps," Real Answers with Steve Russo, *www.realanswers.com/gb.html.*

95 Quoted in Richard Arbanes, *Fantasy and Your Family*. Camp Hill, PA: Christian Publications Inc., 2002, p. 50.

96 Ibid, 46–47.

97 Perry Nodelman, "Ordinary Monstrosity: The World of Goosebumps," *Children's Literature Association Quarterly* vol. 22, no. 3, Fall 1997, 118.

98 Ibid, 119.

99 Quoted in West, "The Horror of R.L. Stine," 40.

100 Timothy Harper, "Why Kids Love Goosebumps: An Interview with Fright-Meister R.L. Stine," *www.familyeducation.com/ article/print/0,1303,1-313,00 .html?obj_gra.*

101 Quoted in Marc Silver, "Horrors! It's R.L. Stine," *U.S. News & World Report*, October 23, 1995, 95.

102 Ibid.

103 Ibid.

104 Quoted on Teen Ink "Interview with Author R.L. Stine," Interview: Author, R.L. Stine.

105 Quoted in Mary B.W. Tabor, "Hints of Horror, Shouts of Protest," *The New York Times*, April 2, 1997, B-6.

106 Ibid.

107 "Harry Potter Series Tops List of Most Challenged Books Four Years in a Row," news release of the American Library Association, January 13, 2003.

108 Quoted in Khalil Abdullah, "Content of Some Books in School Libraries Can Draw Parents' Attention," *Macon Telegraph*, October, 17, 2003.

109 Quoted in "Couple Wants Goosebumps Books Banned from Bay County Schools," Panama City *News Herald*, April 2, 1996.

110 Ibid.

111 Quoted in Tony Simmons, "School Board Won't Ban Goosebumps Books," Panama City *News Herald*, May 9, 1996.

112 Ibid.

113 Quoted in Tony Simmons, "Censorship Watchdog Expects Goosebumps to be Retained," Panama City *News Herald*, March 3, 1996.

114 Quoted in "Couple Wants Goosebumps Books Banned from Bay County Schools."

115 Quoted in Tony Simmons, "Company Rep: Ban Effort is Reaction to Books' Success," Panama City *News Herald*, April 4, 1996.

116 Quoted in "R.L. Stine," Team 10, Literature.

117 Quoted in Simmons, "School Board Won't Ban Goosebumps Books."

118 Quoted in Mary Jane Smetanka, "School Library Won't Bump Goosebumps Off Shelves," Minneapolis *Star-Tribune*, February 5, 1997, 1-A.

119 Quoted in "Pulp Friction," Online NewsHour: "Goosebumps" Children Books February 13, 1997, *www.pbs.org/newshour/ bb/education/february97/ goose_2-13.html*.

120 Quoted in Susan Seibel, "Author R.L. Stine Takes His Fright Factor to a Fantasy World," Pittsburgh *Post-Gazette*, October 20, 2001.

121 R.L. Stine. *Don't Forget Me* (New York: HarperCollins, 2000), introductory page.

122 Ibid., 60.

123 Quoted in Seibel, "Author R.L. Stine Takes His Fright Factor to a Fantasy World."

124 Quoted in "Laura Bush Plugs Press Freedom," *Moscow Times*, October 2, 2003, 3.

125 R.L. Stine, *Who Let the Ghosts Out?* (New York: Delacorte Press, 2004), 25–26.

126 "Who Let the Ghosts Out? Have You Met My Ghoulfriend?" *Washington Post*, October 24, 2004.

1943 Robert Lawrence Stine born on October 8 in Columbus, Ohio; his family soon moves to the nearby suburb of Bexley.

1961 Graduates from high school; enrolls at Ohio State University.

1962 Named editor of *Sundial*, Ohio State University's literary magazine.

1965 Graduates from Ohio State University and accepts a job as a middle school teacher.

1966 Leaves his teaching job and heads to New York City; rents a tiny apartment in Greenwich Village and finds various work as a writer.

1968 Joins the staff of *Junior Scholastic* magazine and later becomes editor of *Bananas*, a humor magazine imprint under Scholastic Incorporated for young people.

1978 Publishes his first book, *How to be Funny: An Extremely-Silly Guidebook*, under the name Jovial Bob Stine.

1986 Writes *Blind Date*, his first suspense novel, using the name R.L. Stine.

1989 Accepts a job as head writer on the cable television show *Eureeka's Castle*; launches the Fear Street series with publication of *The New Girl*.

1992 Publishes *Welcome to Dead House*, the first book in the Goosebumps series.

1995 Publishes *Superstitious*, his lone book for adult readers.

2000 *Guinness Book of World Records* proclaims the Goosebumps series the best-selling children's book series of all time; *Don't Forget Me*, the first title in The Nightmare Room series, is published.

2003 Visits Russia with First Lady Laura Bush as an ambassador to spread literacy; publishes *Dangerous Girls*.

2004 Participates in the Library of Congress National Book Festival; release of *Who Let the Ghosts Out?* and *Have You Met My Ghoulfriend?*, the first two books in the Mostly Ghostly series.

2005 Release of Mostly Ghostly books *One Night in Doom House*, *Little Camp of Horrors*, *Freaks and Shrieks*, *Ghouls Gone Wild*, and *Let's Get This Party Haunted!*

BLIND DATE

R.L. Stine's first suspense novel for young people became an immediate bestseller. Kerry Hart is having a tough time at school and home. He has just been kicked off the football team. His mother has walked out on the family. Kerry's father is distant and has no time for him. His older brother is in a mental institution. What's more, Kerry harbors a dark secret of his own. And then a beautiful new student named Mandy walks into his life, but Kerry soon learns that she is only adding to his troubles.

DANGEROUS GIRLS

R.L. Stine's series for older teens begins with *Dangerous Girls*, which tells the story of Destiny and Livvy Weller, twin sisters, who return from summer camp and discover they have become vampires.

DON'T FORGET ME

The first book in The Nightmare Room series focuses on the story of Danielle Warner, who believes she has hypnotized her little brother Peter into forgetting everything he knows. Instead, Danielle learns that she and Peter are living in the Forget-Me House, and she must figure out a way to save Peter and herself from becoming the forgotten ones.

HOW TO BE FUNNY: AN EXTREMELY-SILLY GUIDEBOOK

R.L. Stine's first published book. Written under the name Jovial Bob Stine, the author gives his readers tips on how to stumble into a classroom, how to tell jokes everyone has heard before, how to eat soup with a fork, how to walk funny, and dozens of other ways to make people laugh.

THE NEW GIRL

Shadyside High School gymnast Cory Brooks finds himself obsessed with Anna Corwin, the beautiful new girl in school. As Cory pursues Anna, he finds her slowly warming to his charms, and yet he can't help but feel his relationship with Anna just isn't quite right. For starters, Anna's brother Brad tries to break up their relationship. And then, Anna keeps disappearing, then turning up in the most unusual places. Finally, people keep telling Cory that Anna is dead. *The New Girl* was R.L. Stine's first novel in the Fear Street series, which eventually featured more than 100 books.

WELCOME TO DEAD HOUSE

The first book in the landmark Goosebumps series, *Welcome to Dead House* tells the story of Amanda and Josh Benson, who move to the dreary town of Dark Falls, where they discover the whole town is inhabited by zombies. Amanda and Josh outsmart the zombies and save their parents.

WHO LET THE GHOSTS OUT?

The first book in the Mostly Ghostly series follows Nicky and Tara Roland as they discover they are ghosts. Soon, they meet Max Doyle, the school nerd, who helps them find out how they died and what happened to their parents. Meanwhile, the evil spirit, Phears, begins his hunt for Nicky and Tara.

WRITING AS JOVIAL BOB STINE

1978 *How to Be Funny: An Extremely-Silly Guidebook; The Absurdly Silly Encyclopedia and Flyswatter*

1979 *The Complete Book of Nerds*

1980 *The Dynamite Do-It-Yourself Pen Pal Kit; Dynamite's Funny Book of the Sad Facts of Life; Going Out! Going Steady! Going Bananas!; The Pig's Book of World Records; The Sick of Being Sick Book* (with Jane Stine)

1981 *Bananas Looks at TV; The Beast Handbook; The Cool Kids' Guide to Summer Camp* (with Jane Stine); *Gnasty Gnomes*

1982 *Don't Stand in the Soup; Bored With Being Bored!: How to Beat the Boredom Blahs* (with Jane Stine)

1983 *Blips!: The First Book of Video Game Funnies; Everything You Need to Survive: Brothers and Sisters* (with Jane Stine); *Everything You Need to Survive: Homework* (with Jane Stine); *Everything You Need to Survive: Money Problems* (with Jane Stine); *Everything You Need to Survive: First Dates* (with Jane Stine)

1985 *Jovial Bob's Computer Joke Book*

1986 *Miami Mice; One Hundred and One Silly Monster Jokes; The Doggone Dog Joke Book*

1989 *Pork and Beans: Play Date; Ghostbusters II Storybook*

1990 *The Amazing Adventures of Me, Myself, and I*

WRITING AS R.L. STINE
Young Adult Novels

1986 *Blind Date*

1987 *Twisted*

1988 *Broken Date*

1989 *The Baby-Sitter*

1990 *Phone Calls; How I Broke Up With Ernie; Curtains; The Boyfriend; Beach Party*

1991 *Snowman; The Girlfriend; Baby-Sitter II*

1992 *Beach House; Hit and Run*

1993 *Hitchhiker; Baby-Sitter III; The Dead Girlfriend; Halloween Night*

1994 *Call Waiting; Halloween Night II*

1995 *Baby-Sitter IV*

Fear Street series

1989 *The New Girl*

1990 *The Surprise Party; The Stepsister; Missing; Halloween Party; The Wrong Number*

1991 *The Sleepwalker; Ski Weekend; Silent Night; The Secret Bedroom; The Overnight; Lights Out; Haunted; The Fire Game*

1992 *The Knife; Prom Queen; First Date; The Best Friend*

1993 *Sunburn; The Cheater*

1994 *The New Boy; Bad Dreams; The Dare; Double Date; The First Horror; The Mind Reader; One Evil Summer; The Second Horror; The Third Horror; The Thrill Club*

1995 *College Weekend; Final Grade; The Stepsister 2; Switched; Truth or Dare; Wrong Number 2*

1996 *What Holly Heard; The Face; Secret Admirer; The Perfect Date; The Boy Next Door; Night Games*

1997 *Runaway; Killer's Kiss; All-Night Party; The Rich Girl; Cat; Fear Hall: The Beginning; Fear Hall: The Conclusion*

Fear Street Super Chiller series

1991 *Party Summer*

1992 *Goodnight Kiss; Silent Night*

1993 *Broken Hearts; Silent Night II*

1994 *The Dead Lifeguard*

1995 *Bad Moonlight; Dead End; New Year's Party*

1996 *Silent Night III; Goodnight Kiss II*

1997 *High Tide*

Fear Street Cheerleaders series

1992 *The First Evil; The Second Evil; The Third Evil; The Evil Lives*

1994 *The New Evil*

Fear Street Seniors series

1998 *Let's Party; Fight Team, Fight; The Gift; Thirst; No Answer; Sweetheart; Evil Heart; Last Chance*

1999 *Spring Break; Wicked; In Too Deep; Prom Date; Graduation Day*

New Fear Street series

1999　*The Stepbrother; Camp Out; The Bad Girl; Scream, Jennifer, Scream*

99 Fear Street series

1994　*The First Horror; The Second Horror; The Third Horror*

Fear Street Saga

1993　*The Betrayal; The Secret; The Burning*

1996　*A New Fear; House of Whispers*

1997　*The Hidden Evil; Daughters of Silence; Children of Fear; Dance of Death; Heart of the Hunter; The Awakening Evil*

1999　*Chamber of Fear; Circle of Fire; One Last Kiss; Faces of Terror; Hand of Power; Door of Death*

Ghosts of Fear Street series

1995　*Hide and Shriek; Who's Been Sleeping In My Grave?; The Attack of the Aqua Apes*

1996　*The Ooze; Revenge of the Shadow People; The Bugman Lives; How to Be a Vampire; Nightmare in 3-D; Stay away from the Treehouse; Eye of the Fortuneteller; Fright Knight; The Boy Who Ate Fear Street; Night of the Werecat; Body Switchers from Outer Space; Fright Christmas*

1997　*Don't Ever Get Sick at Granny's; House of a Thousand Screams; Camp Fear Ghouls; Three Evil Wishes; Spell of the Screaming Jokers; The Creature From Club Lagoona; Field of Screams; Why I'm Not Afraid of Ghosts; Monster Dog; Halloween Bugs Me!; Go To Your Tomb—Right Now!; Parents from the 13th Dimension*

1998　*Hide and Shriek II; Tale of the Blue Monkey; I Was a Sixth-Grade Zombie; Escape of the He-Beast; Caution: Aliens at Work; Attack of the Vampire Worms; Horror Hotel: The Vampire Checks In; Horror Hotel: Ghost in the Guest Room; Funhouse of Doctor Freek*

Cataluna Chronicles

1995　*The Evil Moon; The Dark Secret; The Deadly Fire*

Goosebumps series

1992　*Welcome to Dead House; Stay out of the Basement; Monster Blood; Say Cheese and Die!*

1993   *The Curse of the Mummy's Tomb; Let's Get Invisible; Night of the Living Dummy; The Girl Who Cried Monster; Welcome to Camp Nightmare; The Ghost Next Door; The Haunted Mask; Piano Lessons Can Be Murder; The Werewolf of Fever Swamp; You Can't Scare Me; Be Careful What You Wish For*

1994   *One Day at Horrorland; Why I'm Afraid of Bees; Monster Blood 2; Deep Trouble; The Scarecrow Walks at Midnight; Go Eat Worms!; Ghost Beach; Return of the Mummy; Attack of the Mutant; My Hairiest Adventure*

1995   *Phantom of the Auditorium; Night in Terror Tower; The Cuckoo Clock of Doom; Monster Blood 3; It Came from Beneath the Sink!; The Night of the Living Dummy 2; The Barking Ghost; The Horror at Camp Jellyjam; Revenge of the Lawn Gnomes; A Shocker on Shock Street; The Haunted Mask 2; The Headless Ghost; The Abominable Snowman of Pasadena*

1996   *How I Got My Shrunken Head; Night of the Living Dummy 3; Bad Hare Day; Egg Monsters from Mars; The Beast from the East; Say Cheese and Die—Again!; Ghost Camp; How to Kill a Monster; Legend of the Lost Legend; Attack of the Jack-O'-Lanterns; Vampire Breath; Calling All Creeps!*

1997   *Beware the Snowman; How I Learned to Fly; Chicken, Chicken; Don't Go to Sleep!; The Blob That Ate Everyone; The Curse of Camp Cold Lake; My Best Friend is Invisible; Deep Trouble II; The Haunted School; Werewolf Skin; I Live in Your Basement!; Monster Blood 4*

Goosebumps Presents series

1996   *The Girl Who Cried Monster; Welcome to Camp Nightmare*

Give Yourself Goosebumps series

1995   *Escape from the Carnival of Horrors; Tick Tock, You're Dead; Trapped in Bat Wing Hall*

1996   *The Deadly Experiments of Dr. Eeek; Night in Werewolf Woods; Beware of the Purple Peanut Butter; Under the Magician's Spell; The Curse of the Creeping Coffin; The Knight in Screaming Armor; Diary of a Mad Mummy; Deep in the Jungle of Doom; Welcome to the Wicked Wax Museum*

1997   *Scream of the Evil Genie; The Creepy Creations of Professor Shock; Please Don't Feed the Vampire; Secret Agent Grandma; Little Comic Shop of Horrors; Attack of the Beastly Babysitter; Escape from Camp Run for Your Life; Toy Terror: Batteries Included; The Twisted Tale of Tiki Island*

1998 *Return to the Carnival of Horrors; Zapped in Space; Lost in Stinkeye Swamp; Shop Till You Drop . . . Dead; Alone in Snakebite Canyon; Checkout Time at the Dead-End Hotel; Night of a Thousand Claws; You're Plant Food!; Werewolf of Twisted Tree Lodge; It's Only a Nightmare!*

1999 *It Came from the Internet; Elevator to Nowhere; Hocus-Pocus Horror; Ship of Ghouls; Escape from Horror House; Into the Twister of Terror; Scary Birthday to You!; Zombie School*

2000 *Danger Time; All-Day Nightmare*

Give Yourself Goosebumps Special Edition

1998 *Into the Jaws of Doom; Return to Terror Tower; Trapped in the Circus of Fear; One Night in Payne House*

1999 *The Curse of Cave Creatures; Revenge of the Body Squeezers; Trick or . . . Trapped; Weekend at Poison Lake*

Goosebumps 2000 series

1998 *Cry of the Cat; Bride of the Living Dummy; Creature Teacher; Invasion of the Body Squeezers Part 1; Invasion of the Body Squeezers Part 2; I Am Your Evil Twin; Revenge R Us; Fright Camp; Are You Terrified Yet?; Headless Ghost*

1999 *Headless Halloween; Attack of the Graveyard Ghouls; Brain Juice; Return to Horrorland; Jekyll and Heidi; Scream School; The Mummy Walks; The Werewolf in the Living Room; Horrors of the Black Ring; Return to Ghost Camp; Be Afraid—Be Very Afraid; The Haunted Car; Full Moon Fever; Slappy's Nightmare; Earth Geeks Must Go!; Scream School #15*

2000 *Ghost in the Mirror*

Goosebumps Short Story Anthologies

1994 *Tales to Give You Goosebumps*

1995 *More Tales to Give You Goosebumps*

1997 *Even More Tales to Give You Goosebumps; Still More Tales to Give You Goosebumps; More and More Tales to Give You Goosebumps; More and More and More Tales to Give You Goosebumps*

Space Cadet series

1991 *Jerks in Training; Losers in Space*

1992 *Bozos on Patrol*

Juvenile series

1982   *The Time Raider*

1983   *The Golden Sword of Dragonwalk*

1984   *Horrors of the Haunted Museum; Instant Millionaire; Through the Forest of Twisted Dreams*

1985   *The Badlands of Hark; The Invaders of Hark; Demons of the Deep; Challenge of the Wolf Knight; James Bond in Win, Place, or Die; Conquest of the Time Master*

1986   *Cavern of Phantoms; Mystery of the Impostor; Golden Girl and the Vanishing Unicorn*

1994   *The Beast*

1995   *The Beast 2*

Indiana Jones series

1984   *Indiana Jones and the Curse of Horror Island; Indiana Jones and the Giants of Silver Tower*

1985   *Indiana Jones and the Cult of the Mummy's Crypt*

1987   *Indiana Jones and the Ape Slaves of Howling Island*

G.I. Joe series

1986   *Operation: Deadly Decoy; Operation: Mindbender*

1987   *Serpentor and the Mummy Warrior*

1988   *Jungle Raid; Siege of Serpentor*

Other books

1995   *Superstitious*

1997   *It Came from Ohio: My Life as a Writer* (with Joe Arthur)

1999   *Nightmare Hour*

2000   *Nightmare Hour: Time for Terror; Hotel Horror #1; Hotel Horror #2; The 13th Warning; The Adventures of Shrinkman; The Creatures from Beyond Beyond; My Alien Parents; Three Faces of Me*

2001   *The Haunting Hour: Chills in the Dead of Night; When Good Ghouls Go Bad*

2002   *Beware! R.L. Stine Picks His Favorite Scary Stories; Haunting House: Ten New Stories by R.L. Stine*

2003   *Haunted Lighthouse; The Sitter*

2004   *Eye Candy*

Nightmare Room series

2000 *Don't Forget Me!*; *Liar, Liar*; *Dear Diary, I'm Dead*; *Locker 13*; *My Name is Evil*

2001 *Shadow Girl*; *The Howler*; *Camp Nowhere*; *They Call Me Creature*; *Full Moon Halloween*; *Scare School*; *Visitors*; *Thrillology #1: Fear Games*; *Thrillology #2: What Scares You Most?*; *Thrillology #3: No Survivors*

Rotten School series

2005 *Rotten School #1: The Big Blueberry Barf-Off*; *Rotten School #2: The Great Smelling Bee*

Dangerous Girls series

2003 *Dangerous Girls*

2004 *The Taste of Night*

Mostly Ghostly series

2004 *Have You Met My Ghoulfriend?*; *Who Let the Ghouls Out?*

2005 *Freaks and Shrieks*; *Let's Get This Party Haunted!*; *Ghouls Gone Wild*; *Little Camp of Horrors*; *One Night in Doom House*

Fear Street Nights series

2005 *Moonlight Secrets*; *Midnight Games*; *Darkest Dawn*

AMANDA BENSON

Amanda and her brother Josh are the main characters in *Welcome to Dead House*, the first book in the Goosebumps series. Amanda keeps seeing creepy kids inside the family's new home in Dark Falls, while Josh wonders why their dog Petey is acting so strangely; together, they figure out the town is inhabited by zombies.

DEXTER BREWSTER, HARRISON BABBLE, AND WILMA WALLABY

The three characters are among the class clowns who give tips to readers in R.L. Stine's first book, *How to be Funny: An Extremely-Silly Guidebook*. All three characters share their secrets for how to enter a room: Brewster walks in backwards, Wallaby does the "bump and spill," and Babble—the winner of 17 awards for classroom disruption—stumbles into the room, invariably ending up with his head in the wastebasket.

CORY BROOKS

He is Shadyside High School's star gymnast, but whenever Anna Corwin walks by he turns into Shadyside High's biggest klutz. In *The New Girl*, Cory finds himself overwhelmed by Anna's beauty, but as their relationship progresses he starts learning that Anna is harboring a dark secret.

KERRY HART

The main character of *Blind Date* is wrongly accused of purposely breaking the leg of his team's star quarterback. He must endure beatings from other students, vandalism to his car, and threatening phone calls that are made all hours of the night. Just when things seem darkest, Kerry finds himself on a blind date with Mandy, a new student at Paul Revere High School.

DANIELLE WARNER

Danielle is the featured character in *Don't Forget Me*, the first book in The Nightmare Room series. Danielle believes she has hypnotized her brother, but soon learns that the Warner home is under a curse that makes everyone who lives there forget everything.

NICKY AND TARA ROLAND, AND MAX DOYLE

The reader meets the three main characters in the Mostly Ghostly series in the first book, *Who Let the Ghosts Out?* Nicky and Tara enlist Max to help them find out why they are ghosts and stop the plans of the evil spirit named Phears.

DESTINY AND LIVVY WELLER

The two sisters are at the center of the *Dangerous Girls* books. Destiny struggles to free them both from the curse of vampirism, but Livvy finds herself drawn into the dark world of the undead.

1990 *Eureeka's Castle*, the cable television show whose writing staff was helmed by R.L. Stine, received the Cable Ace Award as Best Children's Show.

1994 Named the best-selling author in America by *USA Today*.

1997 Recipient of the Ohio State University Humanities Alumni Society Award for Distinction, which cited his accomplishment as "the most productive writer in publishing history."

1999 Recipient of the Ohioana Library Association Lifetime Achievement Award, presented to Ohioans who have made significant contributions to literature; *Nightmare Hour* earns the Disney Adventures Kids' Choice Award for Best Horror/Mystery Book.

2000 Certified by *Guinness Book of World Records* as the best-selling children's author in history; *Locker 13* earns the Disney Adventure Kids' Choice Award as Best Horror-Mystery Book.

2001 Inaugurated the Florida Celebration of Reading program. Also, *Publishers Weekly* listed 46 books in the Goosebumps series among the 565 best-selling children's books of all time.

2002 First recipient of the Free Library of Philadelphia Champion of Reading Award.

2003 Member of a delegation headed by First Lady Laura Bush that visited Russia to promote literacy and freedom of speech.

2004 Featured author in the National Book Festival in Washington sponsored by the Library of Congress; *Dangerous Girls* selected a Book for the Teen Age by the New York Public Library Books for the Teen Age, and a Quick Pick for Reluctant Readers by the American Library Association.

Abanes, Richard. *Fantasy and Your Family: A Closer Look at The Lord of the Rings, Harry Potter and Magick in the Modern World.* Camp Hill, PA: Christian Publications, 2002.

"An Interview With the World's Best-Selling Children's Author, R.L. Stine," R.L. Stine–HarperChildrens, *www.harperchildrens.com/ catalog/author_interview_xml.asp?authorid=14471.*

Deutsch, Laura. "R.L. Stine on Why Writing Doesn't Have to be Scary," *Writing*, September 2004.

Gray, Paul. "Carnage: An Open Book," *Time* vol. 142, no. 5, August 2, 1993.

Harper, Timothy. "Why Kids Love Goosebumps: An Interview with Fright-Meister R.L. Stine," *www.familyeducation.com/article/print/ 0,1303,1-313,00.html?obj_gra.*

Jones, Patrick. *What's So Scary About R.L. Stine?* Lanham, MD: Scarecrow Press, 1998.

"Laura Bush Plugs Press Freedom," *Moscow Times*, October 2, 2003.

Moore, Scott. "Plenty of Skeletons in R.L. Stine's Closet," *Los Angeles Times*, October 3, 2000.

Nodelman, Perry. "Ordinary Monstrosity: The World of Goosebumps," *Children's Literature Association Quarterly* vol. 22, no. 3, Fall 1997.

Peacock, Scot, ed. "R.L. Stine," *Contemporary Authors New Revision Series* vol. 109. Farmington Hills, MI: Gale Group, 2002.

———. "R.L. Stine," *Something About the Author* vol. 129. Farmington Hills, MI: Gale Group, 2002.

"Pulp Friction," Online NewsHour: "Goosebumps" Children Books February 13, 1997, *www.pbs.org/newshour/bb/education/february97/ goose_2-13.html.*

"R.L. Stine: A Chat with the Best-Selling Children's Author," CNN— Chatpage—Books, *www.cnn.com/COMMUNITY/transcripts/stine.html.*

"R.L. Stine," Team 10, Literature, *www.cognivision.com/timecapsule61/ timecapsule61/team_10_literature.htm.*

Rodrigues, Tracy, "Meeting the Man Behind the Nightmare Room," Time for Kids | Specials, *www.timeforkids.com/TFK/specials/white/ 0,6406,176520,00.html.*

Roginski, Jim. *Behind the Covers: Interviews with Authors and Illustrators of Books for Children and Young Adults.* Littleton, CO: Libraries Unlimited, 1985.

Russo, Steve. "Goosebumps," *Real Answers with Steve Russo*, *www.realanswers.com/gb.html*.

Seibel, Susan. "Author R.L. Stine Takes His Fright Factor to a Fantasy World," Pittsburgh *Post-Gazette*, October 20, 2001.

Silver, Marc. "Horrors! It's R.L. Stine," *U.S. News & World Report*, October 23, 1995.

Stine, R.L., "How to Write Your Own Give Yourself Goosebumps Books," Creature Feature, *www.scholastic.com/goosebumps/books/stine/writeown.htm*.

Stine, R.L. and Joe Arthur, *It Came from Ohio! My Life as a Writer*. New York: Scholastic Inc., 1997.

Teen Ink. "Interview with Author R.L. Stine," Interview: Author, R.L. Stine, *http://teenink.com/Past/2001/June/Interviews/RLStine.html*.

Telgen, Diane, ed. "R.L. Stine," *Something About the Author* vol. 76. Detroit, MI: Gale Group, 1994.

West, Diane. "The Horror of R.L. Stine," *American Educator* vol. 19, no. 3, Fall 1995.

"Where Do You Get Your Ideas," Creature Feature, *www.scholastic.com/goosebumps/books/stine/ideas.htm*.

"Who Let the Ghosts Out? Have You Met My Ghoulfriend?" *Washington Post*, October 24, 2004.

Cohen, Joel. *R.L. Stine.* San Diego: Lucent Books, 2000.

Holtze, Sally Holmes. Editor. *Seventh Book of Junior Authors & Illustrators.* New York: H.W. Wilson Company: 1996.

Meister, Cari. *R.L. Stine.* Edina, MN: Abdo Publishing, 2001.

Middleton, Haydn. *R.L. Stine.* Portsmouth, NH: Heinemann Educational Books, 2000.

Wheeler, Jill C. *R.L. Stine.* Edina, MN: Abdo & Daughters, 1996.

www.ala.org/ala/oif/bannedbooksweek/bannedbooksweek.htm
[The official Internet page for Banned Books Week is maintained by the American Library Association. Banned Books Week is scheduled annually for the last week in September. Libraries and booksellers participate by prominently displaying for lending or sale the books that have been taken out of class- rooms or school and public library shelves throughout the country. Entering the terms "banned books" or "book censorship" into an Internet search engine can provide the student with many on-line resources on the issue.]

www.scholastic.com/goosebumps/
[The official Goosebumps website includes a biography of R.L. Stine and cover photos of many of the Goosebumps books. Readers can vote for their favorite Goosebumps ghoul, print out T-shirt art, and learn how to make some Goosebumps recipes. These recipes include Bloody Brain Salad, Spicy Deviled Eyeballs, and a Go Eat Worms Sandwich. Stine also gives writing tips to his readers.]

www.thenightmareroom.com/
[Visitors are welcomed by an audio message from R.L. Stine, who asks if they dare to enter The Nightmare Room. Stine's fans can download excerpts from the books as well as a screen saver, and read an on-line story. They can also participate in an interactive story, which changes according to the options they select at different points in the narrative.]

www.randomhouse.com/kids/mostlyghostly/
[Brief descriptions of the Mostly Ghostly books are available at the website maintained by the series publisher. Visitors can also download Mostly Ghostly computer games, screen savers, and wallpaper.]

www.gvshp.org
[Visitors can read about the history of Greenwich Village, New York, on this Internet site maintained by the Greenwich Village Society for Historic Preservation. For more information on the colorful Manhattan neighborhood, the words "Greenwich Village" can be entered into an Internet search engine.]

www.bexleymain.com

> *[News about R.L. Stine's hometown of Bexley, Ohio, is available on this Internet site maintained by the city of Bexley and its chamber of commerce. Visitors can read a history of Bexley and keep up with current events posted on an on-line calendar.]*

ABC television, 81
Absurdly Silly Encyclopedia and Flyswatter, The, 48
Adventures in Horror, (magazine), 40
Adventures of Huckleberry Finn, The, (Twain), 88
Adventures of Pinocchio, (Collodi), 14–15
Affabee, Eric, (pseudonym), 48
and G.I. Joe books, 42
Alice, (series), Naylor, 88
All New Bob Stine Giggle Book, (magazine), 23
American Civil Liberties Union, 90, 91
American Educator, (magazine), 76
American Library Association, (ALA), 88, 89–90
Angier, Naomi, 84
Anoka-Hennepin School District, 95
Arbanes, Richard, 79
Arthur, (series), Brown, 100
Arthur, Joe, 29–30
Asimov, Isaac, 26
Attack of the Mutant, 80

Baby-Sitter, The, 52, 54
Baby-Sitters Club, (series), Lerangis, 100
Bananas, (magazine), 44, 48
Banned Books Week, 88
Barking Ghost, The, 92
Bar Mitzvah, 25
Bat Mitzvah, 25
Bay County School Board, 91, 92, 94–95
Beatles, 39
Beat writers
challenged authority, 38
Bexley, Ohio, 10, 11, 20, 21, 44
Bill of Rights, 86, 89
Blind Date, 51, 56
on best-seller list, 53
and social issues, 57
story of, 52, 53

Block, Lawrence, 102
Blue, Zachary, (pseudonym), 48
Bobbsey Twins, (series), 89
Bob Stein Presents, 29
Bony Fingers From the Grave, (story), 40
Bored With Being Bored! How to Beat the Boredom Blahs, 48
Boston, 86
Bova, Ben, 102
Boy Scouts of America, 89
Bozos on Patrol, 94
Bradbury, Ray, 26, 64
Brain Juice, 67, 101
Brinkley, Douglas, 102
Brown, Marc, 100
Bush, Laura, 96, 100–101, 102

Caesar, Sid, 28
Came from Ohio: My Life as a Writer, It, 27, 47
Campbell, Glen, 39
Caniff, Milton, 29
Catcher in the Rye, The, (Salinger), 88
Censorship, 87, 88, 91, 97
Children's Literature Association Quarterly, 79
Clinton, Kip, 91, 92–93, 94–95
Clinton, Lisa, 91, 92–93, 94–95
CNN, 69
Collodi, Carlo, 14–15
Color Purple, The, (Walker), 88
Columbus, (Ohio), 11, 20, 21
Complete Book of Nerds, The, 48
Corso, Gregory, 38
Country and Western Music, (magazine), 39
Crawford County School Board, 90
C-SPAN, 95

Dangerous Girls, (series), 17, 102
Dear Diary, I'm Dead, 100
Dime novels, 89

Don't Forget Me, 97–98, 103
   plot twists in, 99–100
Double Date, 90
Dr. Seuss, 60
Dutton, E.P., (publisher), 45
Dylan Bob, 38

Elliott, Bob, 28
Eloquent Insanity, 29
Eureeka's Castle, (puppet show)
   aired on cable T.V., 47
Everything You Need to Survive:
   Brothers and Sisters, 48
Everything You Need to Survive:
   First Dates, 48
Everything You Need to Survive:
   Homework, 48

Fall into Darkness, 90
Family Education Network, 82
Fantasy and Your Family, (Arbanes),
   79
Farmer's Market, 21
Father Elijah, (series), O'Brien, 79
Fear Street, (series), 17, 56, 57, 61,
   64, 80, 89–90, 105
   scary books, 50, 54, 55
Feiwel, Jean
   on asking Stine to write a horror
      novel, 48–49, 51
15, (magazine), 39
First Evil
   theme of, 56–57
First Scream, 71–72
Florida Coalition Against
   Censorship, 93
Fox Family, 81
Fox Kids cable television, 81
Freedom of Speech, 86
From Here to Insanity, 23, 24

Gainesville, Florida, 90
G.I. Joe, (books), 42, 48
Ginsberg, Allen, 38
Girl Who Cried Monster, The, 68

Give Yourself Goosebumps, (series),
   60
Goodnight Kiss, 58
   excerpt from, 70
Goosebumps, 17, 59, 60, 64, 66,
   79–80, 84, 92–93, 94, 95, 98,
   105
   best selling of all time, 61
   censoring of, 89–90, 91–96
   series of books, 56
   and Television series, 81
Goulding, Ray, 28
Green Eggs and Ham, (Dr, Seuss),
   60
Greenwich Village, 36, 37, 63
Guinness Book of World Records,
   61

Hah, for Maniacs Only!, 23
Hardy Boys, (series), 89
Harper, Timothy, 82, 84
Harry Potter Books, (Rowling),
   60, 88
Haunted Lighthouse, 81
Haunted Mask, The, 58, 66, 92
Have You Met My Ghoulfriend?,
   105
Hawkins, Helma, 84
Horror of R.L., Stine, The, (West),
   76
How to be Funny: An Extremely
   Silly Guidebook, 45
How to be Funny in School,
   (chapter), 45–46
   sales of, 48
How I Broke Up With Ernie, 101

Indiana Jones, 42, 48
Innersanctum, (radio), 13
Institutional Investor, (magazine),
   38

Jackson's, The, 39
James Bond, 42, 48
Jerks in Training, 94

Jones, Tom, 39
Jovial Bob's Computer Joke Book, 48
Jovial Bob Stine, 31, 45
Junior Scholastic, (magazine), 41, 42, 60–61

Kerouac, Jack, 38
Kovacs, Ernie, 28

Lantern, (student newspaper), 33
Lerangis, Peter, 100–101
Let's Get Invisible
theme of, 18
Liar, Liar, 100, 103
Library of Congress National Book Festival, (2004), 102
Lloyd, Christopher, 81
Locker 13, 100, 103
Losers in Space, 94

Mad, (magazine), 22–23, 44
Maloney, Cynthia, 93–94
Manhattan, 62, 63, 71
Many Loves of Dobie Gillis, The, (Shilman), 28
Mathieson, Franklin, 89
McKean, Michael, 81
Mice and Men, Of, (Steinbeck), 88
Mindswap, (Sheckley), 26
Mod Teen, (magazine), 39
Monster Blood, 67
Mostly Ghostly, (series), 17, 103
Murders in the Rue Morgue, (Poe), 76–77

Nancy Drew books, 84, 89
Naylor, Phyllis Reynolds, 88
New Girl, The, 56
social issues in, 57
story of, 55–56
New York City, 34, 36, 37
New York City University, 36
New Yorker, The, (magazine), 28–29
New York Times Book Review, 78

Nickelodeon, 47
Night of the Living Dummy II, 91–92
Nightmare Room, The, (series), 17, 81, 97–98, 100, 103
Nodelman, Perry
his criticism of Stine, 79–82

Oates, Joyce Carol, 102
O'Brien, Michael, 79
Ohio, 10, 11, 16, 98
Ohio State University, 20, 21, 28, 30, 45
O'Neill, Eugene, 37–38

Panama City, Florida, 91, 92–93
Parachute Press, 41, 48, 54, 57
Phone Calls, 101
Piano Lessons Can Be Murder
theme of, 17
Pigs' Book of World Records, The, 48
Pit and the Pendulum, The, (Poe), 76–77
Poe, Edgar Allan, 64, 74, 76–77
Potter, Beatrix, 60
Publishers Weekly, 60
on *Blind Date*, 53–54
Putina, Lyudmila, 100

Raiders of the Lost Ark, (film), 42, 48
Raven, The, (Poe), 74
Reed, John, 37–38
R.L. Stine's Haunted Lighthouse, (movie), 81
Rolling Stones, 39
Rowling, J.K., 60, 79, 88
Russo, Steven
on Stines's stories, 78–79

Salinger, J.D., 88
Say Cheese and Die!, 81, 92
Scarecrow Walks at Midnight, The, 92
Scholastic Incorporated, 36, 93

School Library Journal, 54
Screenplay, (magazine), 39
Search, (magazine), 43
Senior Scholastic, (magazine), 43
Shadow, The, (radio), 12
Sheckley, Robert, 26
Shepherd, Jean, 28, 64
Shulman, Max, 28
Sick of Being Sick Book, The, 48
Soft Drink Industry, (magazine),
    40–41
Something About the Author, 58
Something Wicked This Way Comes,
    (Bradbury), 26
Space Cadets, (series), 94
Spider–Man, 35
Stay Out of the Basement, 66–67,
    81
Steinbeck, John, 88
Sterling, Rod, 26, 98
Steve Canyon, (comic strip), 29
Stine, Anne, 22, 32
Stine, Lewis, 22, 32
Stine, Matt, 47
    on inspiring his father, 58
Stine, Pamela, 22, 32
Stine, R.L., 79, 83, 86
    his adventure novels, 48
    the attic, 11–12, 16, 105
    his book tours, 61
    on campaigning for student
        senate President, 32–33
    his characters, 68–70
    connecting with young people,
        43
    and criticized, 74–86
    his defenders, 82–85
    his early years, 11–12, 22, 24,
        25
    a fan of science fiction, 26
    his favorite magazines, 22–23
    his fear, 27
    his guidelines for a story, 68
    and heading to New York, 34,
        35, 36

as head writer for *Eureeka's
    Castle*, 47
on how he writes, 65–66
his ideas, 66–67, 71
his imagination, 12, 13–14
his major, 28
his office, 62, 63–64
and personal favorites, 101
and response to his critics, 85
his success, 17
and teaching, 34, 35
his trip to Moscow, 96, 100–102
Stine, William, 11, 12, 15, 17
Sundial, (literary magazine), 28–29,
    30, 39, 45
    on Girl of the Month, 31, 32
    and Stine joining the staff, 29,
        30
Superstitious, 69
Suspense, (radio), 13
Swilley, Henrietta, 95

Tale of Peter Rabbit, The, (Potter),
    60
Tales from the Crypt, (magazine),
    22–23
Taste of Night, The, 102–103
Tell-Tale Heart, The, (Poe), 76–77
Terr, Leonore, 84
Thompson, Lea, 81
Thurber, James, 28–29
Tolkien, J.R.R., 79
Tucker, Ken, 78, 87
Twain, Mark, 88
Twilight Zone, The, (television),
    26, 98
Twisted, 54
Typewriter, 10, 18–19, 23

United States
    and censorship, 86
Uproarious Utopia, 29
U.S. News and World Report, 84

Vault of Horror, (magazine), 22–23

Waldhorn, Jane, 41, 48, 54
Walker, Alice, 88
Walt Disney Company, 14
Waricha, Joan, 54, 57, 59
Washington Post, 105
WB television, 81
Weekly Standard, The, (magazine),
    75, 76
Weird Al Yankovic, 81
Welcome to Dead House, 81
    theme of, 59–60

West, Diane, 76–78, 82, 87
Whammy, 23, 24
Whistler, The, (radio), 12–13
Who Let the Ghosts Out?,
    103–105
Winter Market, 21–22
Wodehouse, P.G., 28, 64
Writer's block, 64–66

Young writers, 72–73

HAL MARCOVITZ is a journalist who lives in Pennsylvania with his wife Gail and daughters Ashley and Michelle. He is the author of the novel *Painting the White House* as well as more than 60 nonfiction books for young readers. His other titles in the WHO WROTE THAT? series include biographies of authors Will Hobbs and Bruce Coville.